PRAISE FOR MU

'Boss' – Sam Avery – The Learner Parent

'Hilarious moments that will strike a chord with mothers everywhere' – The Daily Mail

'You are bang on with everything. You're the first person who has finally said it' – The Hot Mess Mums

'Funny and frank' – Honest Mum, Vicki Broadbent

'The laugh out loud tales are relatable and raw' – The Natural Parenting Magazine

And what did the mums think?

'Amazing' – Charlotte's Mum

'I'm in stitches. It's all so true' – Ava's Mum

'A reflection of what goes through every mother's mind in that first year'

– Björn and River's Mum

'Brilliantly honest and extremely funny' – Archie's Mum

'So funny, rings true for everyone' – Bella's Mum

'Genuinely loved reading it' – Theo's Mum

'I can relate so well to everything you have written' – Cian's Mum

ISBN: 979-8-648-70337-7

Cover design: Rebecca Oxtoby

MUM'S
THE
WORD

REBECCA OXTOBY

For Isabelle Rose:

There's nobody else I'd let shit

on me

WELCOME TO THE CLUB

So, you're knocked up. Well done. However it happened – IVF, fertility drugs, behind the back of a Wetherspoons – I congratulate you. You're in for a treat. Becoming a mum is a glorious privilege and, lucky for you, I'm here to give you a sneak peek into the slobbery, shit-stained, sleepless world you've signed yourself up to.

My husband, Danny, and I are new parents to Isabelle Rose, born 25.06.2019. She is incredible; a little fluffy-headed milk guzzler with big eyes and the sass of a teenager. She's turned our world upside down in every kind of way.

Before parenthood, I was an enthusiastic career woman, working as the Clinical Lead for Stroke for Speech and Language Therapy at an inner-city hospital.

Now, 8 months in (or 37 weeks, because, as you'll soon realise, all new parents must count in weeks for no reason whatsoever), my enthusiasm peaks at sweeping the kitchen floor with my foot and a tea-towel, or being arsed to spray dry shampoo onto my sick-matted hair.

Disclaimer: in case you hadn't realised, I'm a parenting novice. In fact, I can't even keep plants alive. So, if you're looking for parenting advice (or horticultural advice for that matter) you've wasted a fiver.

So no, this is not a parenting manual. Lord knows I haven't the faintest fuck what I'm doing.

Instead, I'll be revealing the biggest secrets of post-spawn life; the highest of highs, and the bottom-of-the-nappy-bin lows. Because let's face it, it's both ecstasy (not the drug) and misery that makes a mother.

Truthfully, writing this book has been an attempt at preserving my sanity in what has sometimes felt like a very, very long year 'off work' (note: 'off work' is a lie. Just think of it as moving to a new department where your job is unpaid, for 168 hours a week, with no training. Oh, and your boss shits on the floor).

So, grab a seat. Keep your arms, legs and bump inside the vehicle at all times. Oh, and hold on tight, it can be a bit of a rough ride.

A

Accidents

...happen. The initiation ceremony to becoming a parent is actually pretty brutal. Even with the best intentions, you're guaranteed to sob your heart out because you not only woke the baby getting her out of the car seat, but you also accidentally smacked her head off the car roof.

Even months down the line, when you think you've finally cracked it, the kid reminds you that you're completely out of your depth: faceplanting a dirty play-centre floor when you were convinced that she could sit up on her own.

I'm pretty sure I could have started a foodie Instagram account showcasing the culinary delights I've dropped onto her face during a feeding multi-task fail.

But I take comfort in knowing that thankfully it's not just mums who screw up. I took perverse joy in watching Daddy's face drop through his arse when he playfully lifted her into the air and smashed her head on the pendant light in her bedroom (Don't worry, Isabelle was fine. She actually slept through that night – a mother's guide to the Big Bang theory).

But nothing comes close to what happened tonight. I'm pretty sure I'm going to have long-standing PTSD. I'm so sorry Isabelle.

Tonight, Friday 13th March, will be forever etched in my memory.

My brother and his girlfriend came around for tea. 8-month old Isabelle sat patiently in her highchair, listening intently to our conversation and babbling away in response.

As time went by, we decided to move into the living room, so Danny lifted Isabelle from her chair and noticed that one side of her leggings was moist from hip to knee. In his naïve and child-free state, my brother offered to change what he thought would be just a wet nappy.

Bless.

I sat by Isabelle's head to give him morale support as he removed her pants. It was evident that he was shocked at the amount of crap seeping from the side of the 'leak-free' pull-ups, so to further prove the point, I held the shit-filled leggings out to showcase the mass of poo inside them.

In slow motion, the contents fell from the leggings and onto my beautiful daughter's open-mouthed face.

I dropped shit in her mouth.

I'm so sorry baby girl.

ARGUMENTS

A baby brings more joy than you could ever imagine. But along with cooing, lullabies and snuggles comes exhaustion like you've never felt before. And that, my friend, is a catalyst for a fight.

Before Isabelle, I genuinely liked my husband. Not all the time, but I could bear the sound of him breathing and didn't want to shove a Tommee Tippee bottle up his arse every time he spoke.

Nowadays - since that tiny lodger moved in - we can't stop bickering, and it drives me mad.

First off, that man is adamant that he is more exhausted than me, and yes, he works full-time, but 24/7 with a drooling, sleep-deprived little monster sucking on your tits until they are raw is hardly a holiday (though it does sound a lot like Kavos 2010).

And then we have the night feeds. They're notoriously tough going, yet rather than acting like grown adults and agreeing some kind of turn-taking system, we both lie completely still in bed whenever she cries; waiting with baited breath in the hope that the other will cave first.

Occasionally, I'll even let out a snore or a bit of dribble for authenticity. It's all in vain though, as, by some strange coincidence, it's almost always Mama who is left holding the baby. Literally.

Isn't it funny how my darling husband just cannot hear the screaming cries of a hungry baby bellowing through an amplifier next to his face, but he awakens at the sound of my head lifting from the pillow?

'Oh, oh [rubbing his bastard eyes] is she awake? Are you getting her babe?'

Arsehole.

Of course, I'm onto him, so I get out of bed with the grace of a labouring rhino, which, on occasion, has unfortunately woken Daddy too.

Oops. OK, it doesn't make me less tired and it definitely doesn't get the baby back to sleep any quicker, but it still feels good.

And, before we go there, I'm ready with a nappy sack grenade for the person who suggests 'Mummy should do in the week because Daddy is working'. I'm hardly sunning it up at a Sandals beach resort; I barely have the time to wipe my own arse.

The little point-scoring bickers spanned the first few months of parenthood, and followed every sleep regression (you didn't read the parenting T&Cs either did you? Sleep regression is a child's get-out clause allowing the kid to wake up whenever they fancy in the night, for no reason whatsoever), new tooth, and day when Isabelle was generally being a dick. Those days, and those fights, still rear their ugly heads, like a spot on a first date, or a nursery bill.

After weeks of arguing, my poor husband offered a truce with a beautiful bunch of my favourite freesia – *'oh great thanks, something else to not let die.'*

#prayforDanny

B

BABY BRAIN

At first, I definitely used this as an excuse for, well, pretty much every mistake I'd made whilst pregnant.

Forgotten to put the bins out? Baby brain. Forgotten to send a birthday card? Oops, baby brain. Forgotten to set your alarm for work and turned in 2 hours late? Morning sickness.

It bit me on the arse though when I was unfortunately diagnosed with the condition (thanks to Dr. Google) during my second trimester. I must have caught a pretty nasty dose as it has lasted well into the first year of parenthood.

Since her birth, I've found the remote control in the fridge, left my car door wide open whilst I sat obliviously in a restaurant, and climbed out of the living room window because I'd convinced myself I'd lost my house keys, which, incidentally, were in the living room.

Last Wednesday, I arrived home from an afternoon at the garden centre to find my front door completely ajar.

 Leaving Isabelle safely locked away in the car (windows down, Judge), I called my friend for moral support as I braved walking into what was undoubtedly the aftermath of a burglary.

The friend I chose to call lived in Northern Ireland, so there was fuck all she could do if I was actually confronted with an axe-wielding madman lugging my tele under his arm, but still...

As it turns out, there was no baddie and my TV was safe. I'd simply left the house that morning, put Isabelle in the car and driven off, without even shutting the god damn front door.

What a knob.

Luckily, nothing was taken (not even that bastard stuffed rabbit that whines for a carrot every 20 seconds), it was all just slightly glacial thanks to the gale-force wind running through the hallway. Danny wasn't overly impressed.

These spells of idiocy started with an absolute corker when I was pregnant. In an equally moronic attempt at luring the emergency services, I - the bun-in-the-oven trophy wife - prepared a roast for us both one Sunday evening while Danny was at work. Smug with my efforts, I made a brew and sat in the lounge until he got home.

Rudely, he barely acknowledged me as he walked in. Instead, alerted by a charring scent, he ran straight into the kitchen, where he found a raw chicken perched proudly on top of the stove and a tea towel on fire in the oven.

He cooked after that (every cloud...).

Baby Monitors

I love it when she's awake, but I love it so much more when she's asleep.

Nothing defines 'bliss' like that golden hour when she has finally given it a rest and is out cold in her crib (not dead obviously, just asleep).

Each night I waltz back downstairs, grinning with delight at the thought of my first hot drink of the day (at 8.30pm) and one or two (packets of) chocolate digestives to celebrate us both surviving the day.

The only thing that tarnishes the peace is the distraction of a grainy black and white monitor screen. You see, it's frowned upon to just leave her upstairs without having one eye on what she's up to at all times, even when she's doing fuck all because she is fast asleep. I guess a mother's work is never done.

The problem is, horror films of the noughties have evidently scarred me for life. I can barely look at the monitor without visions of her being pulled leg-first off the screen to her inevitable bloody murder by a paranormal demon.

It's recently been plastered all over the news that hackers can access baby monitors and subsequently spy on your child whilst they sleep. Horrifying, I'm sure. But, if you are a hacker and fancy keeping an eye on her for me so I can watch Black Mirror in peace, please get in touch.

I swear the devices are factory-fitted with phantom cries that set the noise sensor lights off every few hours. Either that or some guy in Japan is sitting at his computer pissing himself laughing at my expense, because someone in that room is crying, and it's not my kid.

If that wasn't enough, my monitor has started switching the screen into blackout mode for just long enough for me to convince myself that there is a man with one hand over the camera and the other smothering her face. I'm adamant that when the screen comes back on her bed will be empty and a ransom note will be pinned to her cot: my absolute worst nightmare as we're saving for the garden to be landscaped.

Belly Button

Ahh a newborn: a perfect little bundle with 10 tiny fingers and 10 tiny toes. A gorgeous mop of thick curly hair and a crusty worm escaping from a hole in her stomach.

Oh yes, the unspoken horror that is a baby's forming belly button.

Every nappy change in that first week was vomit buckaroo: working in stealth mode to avoid knocking the biggest crocodile clip I'd ever seen, attached by rotting flesh to a gaping red crater in my little girl's belly. You never see that shit on a newborn photo shoot.

Finally, on day 5, the bastard thing surrendered and fell onto my arm, and for a second, I debated whether to keep the putrid souvenir.

Gross.

(When I told that story to a co-worker, she smiled awkwardly and admitted that she still has her 5-year-old son's in a box on her vanity desk).

BIRTH

It's inevitable, personal and unpredictable. It's also often completely out of your control. Take it as a heads-up from your kid as to who is the boss from now on. Spoiler alert: it's not you.

Organised, optimistic and completely deluded, I strutted into my 36-week midwife appointment with a laminated birth plan, depicting images of exactly how her arrival would pan out; Coldplay would be whispering 'Paradise' in a darkened room, lit only by scattered (battery-operated) tealight candles.

In amongst them was a serene, calm and collected me: zen-like in a birthing pool, cradled by my husband and using deep breathing techniques to sail through each surge until I met my baby.

Hmm.

Then Isabelle decided to stick her little tush right into my pelvis and declare her escape route bum-first.

Though breech babies can be birthed vaginally (folded up like a clam), my consultant advised that it's safer to get her out of the sunroof in a planned c-section. And whilst I was relieved that I wouldn't have to squeeze out a C-shaped human, and the control freak in me delighted in knowing her birth date weeks in advance (exactly 6 months from Christmas day – the type A personality's dream), the loss of my carefully-planned labour and textbook birth hit me hard.

I'd pictured the waters breaking in a restaurant, the midnight rush to the hospital and the heavy panting in the car, just like in the films. I wanted the contractions, and I really wanted to squeeze Danny's hand so hard that I broke his fingers.

Yet, all of a sudden, it was gone.

Sharing my disappointment with a friend who had birthed her baby naturally a month before, I was reminded that a vaginal birth can go equally tits up. She was offered both forceps (salad tongs) and ventouse (a fucking hoover) at the climax of her 18-hour labour, and she still ended up with stitches, though hers were between her front and back passages. She literally ripped herself a new arsehole.

After that, it made sense to me why midwives tell you to write birth 'preferences' rather than plans. The baby is definitely in control now, you are merely the body from which she will expel herself, whenever and however she fancies (apparently they're worth it, so I've been told).

 Next time, I'm going to write, 'Dad to carry and birth child. Mum will hold his hand and rub his back'.

Body

If there is one thing that pregnancy is almost guaranteed to bring (other than sickness, piles and a baby) it's a couple of extra dress sizes.

Some women are fortunate, with their metabolism and self-control, and then there are girls like me.

Girls that know that eating for two is a myth, but still manage to convince themselves that the baby needs a share bag of Chilli Heatwave Doritos and a 4 pack of Wispa Gold.

Girls who put on 3 stone in 9 months, and only when the baby comes out, realise that they've become more Simply Be than Topshop.

During my pregnancy, I loved to wear fitted tops to flaunt my ever-expanding tum, and though subliminally I probably knew that other bits were expanding too, I found a new body confidence, even when I was waddling round ASDA in a vest top and leggings.

There is something really beautiful about a pregnant woman's body. I guess I just didn't think about what would happen after Isabelle had vacated the building.

Fast forward to 4 months post-partum and I still looked like a deflated airbag with chaffing legs and back fat.

When out shopping alone (a rarity), three separate people made conversation alluding to my 'pregnant' belly.

Of course, I was too mortified to ever tell them that I was due 4 months ago, especially with one hand full of Kit-Kats and a cheese board in the other.

Even Facebook has jumped on the fat-shaming bandwagon, replacing my ASOS targeted ads of old with recommendations for 'chub rub' shorts. Wankers.

I'm sure they're taunting me: every other news story is about a celeb who 'bounced back' into their size 8 jeans. The only thing I've bounced back from is the fridge.

I actually found my new body one of the hardest things to come to terms with. I went from a size 10 to a size 18 in a year, and without the bump, I felt, and still feel, completely lost in my new, saggy skin.

There are so many beautiful post-partum quotes about 'loving your tiger stripes' and living in awe of the miracle that your body has just created.

But truthfully, I hated the new me. I wanted Danny to capture every moment of me with my girl, yet I couldn't bear to look at the woman standing in the picture. She wasn't the confident, slim, proud girl I knew. She was fat, with jiggly arms and her clothes clung to the rolls around her back.

I know that so many people would give their life for this scar and this empty pouch, because it means that they've been given the gift of motherhood. I know because I've been that girl, but while I know that I should embrace the chunk and all that it represents, it will take time for me to recognise myself within this fat suit.

Boobs

Breasts, bosom, boobies, baps. Whatever you call them, they supersize after baby...and I'm talking old Pammy Anderson, page 3 shit (if page 3 models had deep blue veins running across their chest like a map of the Manchester ship canal).

Whilst my pre-pregnancy self would have rejoiced at the mere thought of a cleavage – my breasts had never met one another before Isabelle – the reality isn't nearly as glamorous.

The struggle is particularly real in those first few days, when your milk 'comes in'. They make this sound like an Ocado delivery, but it's not: it doesn't come neatly packaged – there is literally milk pissing up the walls – and there is absolutely no cancelling of your order.

Whether you decide to breast or bottle feed, your breasticles will swell up like steroid-injected melons, full to the brim with milk until they burst. Well, almost.

Bottle feeding mamas are recommended to stuff their bras with cabbage (WTF) in an attempt to ease the swelling and make the milkies go away. But nobody tells you what to do with the cabbage, leading a friend of mine to boil hers and subsequently smell like a post-partum roast dinner.

Alternatively, you can opt to let that teeny tiny new lodger of yours suckle on you until your nips bleed. I jest (kind of).

The initial toe-curling latch pain doesn't last forever (thank Jesus, Mary and Joseph) but it lasts long enough to make you want to throw your beautiful little bundle out of an upstairs window. God bless nipple shields.

4 months down the line and there were still frequent reminders that I was yet to master breastfeeding.

Like the time when Isabelle was younger, and would frequently fall asleep on me whilst feeding on the couch. Enjoying the snuggles, I left her there and dead-scrolled on my phone for 20 minutes, until the window cleaner came knocking for payment.

Sleeping babe in arms, I strolled to the door whilst rooting through my purse for change, not realising that my full breast – nipple and all – was exposed underneath her head.

I only noticed when the ageing gentleman before me looked at her, then down, then dropped his record book and money tin into my porch. If that's how easy strip money is, I'm game.

The titastrophes became more commonplace as I began to venture beyond my front door.

In winter, I attended a 2-hour Baby Choking Prevention session put on by the local college. As standard, Isabelle was due a feed about 30 minutes in, so I subtly whipped one out and latched her on. 60 seconds, and a huge let-down later, she pulled off to catch her breath, and like a sprinkler, I super-soaked her and a couple of nearby toddlers.

Whoops.

I guess the main problem I find with breastfeeding is only you have the breasts.

I was lucky enough to be able to express, but, rather inconveniently, I'm not always in the vicinity of a pump when I'm away from the baby (and let's be honest, the Trafford Centre just isn't the place for a milking).

And whilst my head knows that, my milk plays by the rules of hide and seek and comes out whether I'm ready or not.

3 hours into a rare child-free day out with the girls and I was bursting out of my bra like Hulk with tired eyes. The pain was intense and the bra was damp. Cue milking myself in Chiquitos' toilet: squirting mum juice up the wall and clogging the toilet with the paper I'd used to clean up the mess. And who said motherhood wasn't glamorous?

Maybe it's just me. I'm sure some mothers are classier than I am. Like the ones who follow the handy little tip to wear a bobble on your wrist to remind you which breast to feed from next. You move the bobble after every feed: efficient and subtle in principle, but I can barely remember to change my underwear, or what day it is, so I just stick with a quick grope on each side.

C

Car seat

You best have started your weight training in pregnancy because car seats are heavy, and the weight only increases as the little sod gets bigger.

Thinking back now, I really shouldn't have complained about carrying my 6-week old into soft play next to a woman lugging around 8-month old twins and a toddler. Absolute machine. And you need a master's degree in engineering to figure out how to clip it all together.

I've definitely spent a good 5 minutes or so trying to buckle up a screaming baby, not realising that the kid was only crying because I was continually catching her tummy in the clips.

The game switches to expert mode when the child realises that they can completely resist the seat by feigning rigamortis. The first time they do this will inevitably be when there are no parent and child spaces left so your door is barely open, wedged up against a poorly-parked 19 plate Audi, and you're sweating in a baggy hoody and loaded like a pack horse. I've found that a firm tickle to the belly breaks the board. If not, karate chop and get on with your day.

Those ISOFIX bases are brilliant though; one clunk in and (somehow) she's safe. Only 3 times have we heard the beep of the car seat actually connecting to the base half-way through the journey.

Still, better than forgetting entirely to strap her in when you're out and about in a car that isn't your own. I was so used to clicking in the ISOFIX, it wasn't until we arrived home that I realised that I'd pretty much just placed her on the back seat. She'd have been safer in the boot. Supermum fail 101.

She's just moved into one of those big girl car seats and I'm heartbroken; not because she's growing too fast but because I can't leave the bloody car when she's asleep now. Cue half an hour of silent online shopping on your drive, and scaring the shit out of the postman.

Cellular Blankets

One of the golden nuggets I'd picked up from the 'how not to kill your baby' class was to buy cellular (holey) blankets.

The aim of this is to stop the little monster from self-suffocating in their sleep. You'd think 'not even a kid is stupid enough to smother their own face' but as it turns out, my child only sleeps this way; blanket completely covering her head.

Whilst it's pretty funny watching unsuspecting guests realise that she's no longer on the baby monitor, it means that the 15 non-holey blankets we got given at the baby shower are for decoration only, lest we get into a court case, and who's got time for that?

CLASSES

Flashback to the first day of high school and you can almost imagine how it feels to walk into a Mum and Baby class.

Except, in high school, you didn't have to keep another human fed, happy, and generally alive whilst a bunch of self-righteous arseholes watched on (apart from the time when Mr. Bannister paired me with that really socially-awkward Chinese exchange student).

There are definitely similarities to school though. First off, damn those classes are cliquey. There are the cool mamas who have their shit together, a curly blow and a full face of flawless make up. Their daughters have outfits with matching headbands from places like Zara which are paired with colour-coordinated (and completely useless) shoes.

Those mamas have had a full night's sleep, and don't we all know about it. *'Serengeti [or insert equally obnoxious name] slept for 11 hours last night, she's an angel'.*

And then there's awkward me: sporting designer black bags under my eyes and a spit-matted mum-bun: dressed in my well-worn maternity leggings and a sick-stained baggy hoody.

Isabelle is dressed in George's finest (well she was, but she sharted so now she's in a vestless, mismatched outfit, one size too small, from the bottom of the changing bag). She's kicking off for no reason whatsoever; despite me spending all morning delicately coordinating feeds and sleep so that she wouldn't be a witch for this bastard class.

Walking in with fake confidence, I say 'hi' to my new mum friends, who stare through me and carry on chatting about how Consuela and Ne-coli can count to 10 in French and Spanish at the ripe old age of 18 weeks. Yawn.

The class starts (we waft bits of tinfoil over the babies who, if we're honest, couldn't give two Tombliboos) and the mind-numbing chatter continues. '*Charlamane didn't even look up from writing her thesis whilst having her second lot of injections*', '*Oregano's signed up to do the Great North Run next year*'.

The end of the class was nigh (hallelujah) and it soon became apparent why the Cheshire housewives were on their high horses (metaphorically of course - their actual horses were back at the stables).

They've been here before. They knew what was coming. They had the 12-step dance routines of singalong time down to a T. Why didn't the class organiser send me the choreography beforehand? Some crazy Beyoncé shit to *Wind the bobbin up* (and who the fuck is promoting this child labour?) and they all knew it apart from me.

Worst of all, my kid had finally fallen asleep (after 45 minutes of screaming because she was tired, but not tired enough to actually go the fuck to sleep in the first place), so I had to sing 'to the room' instead, awkwardly making eye contact with the class leader who would zestfully sing back at me.

I found my groove *during Twinkle Twinkle Little Star*, and started to feel a little less like a prat.

That was until we had to say goodbye. Not like a normal 'goodbye see you next week' though, oh no. We went around the class singing to every single one of the twenty-odd kids in there.

Let me teach you the song. All the mamas sing 'goodbye' together and then the mum of the chosen child has to SING their child's name in a Pitch Perfect-esque acapella solo to the room; and whilst I have the body of Fat Amy, I'm no performer.

I wanted the sandpit to swallow me whole. Unsurprisingly, we only went to that group once.

Cleaning

I'm heartbroken to admit it, but there is nothing more futile than trying to keep a house clean with a baby.

Despite all good intentions, there is absolutely no point in scrubbing the kitchen floor; it will be smeared with a mashed banana and porridge medley within the hour.

Fresh bedding is a waste of detergent; it's guaranteed to be spewed on that same night, and don't bother cleaning the toilet; a tired husband's aim is like a jet-spray in a storm.

Yesterday, I found a fluffy orange bit of a Jaffa cake behind the TV. I genuinely have no idea how long it's been there. And no matter what I use, I can't get the Weetabix and blueberry concoction off the highchair. It's cemented the tray to the base so well that I think I'll pitch it to B&Q.

I just don't think that I'm ready to accept that I'm going to live in my own filth for 18 years, but I'm too tight to pay a cleaner, so if you're ever visiting, just leave one of your contact lenses in the car, or bring a mop.

CONVERSATIONS

I love a catch up with the girls. There is nothing better than a good natter with a splash of gossip over afternoon tea (with a Groupon voucher of course, I'm not posh).

It's what we live for.

I couldn't wait for a whole year of socialising and lunching with the ladies – living the high life on maternity leave. Swept away with the thought of coffee catch ups and overpriced cake, I guess I forgot that the kid needs to come with you wherever you go.

And I'll tell you now, you'll find yourself searching for the end of a bottomless brunch when you have a whingey, snot-nosed child in tow.

Maybe that's why I'm so bitter towards the Mum Tribe who seem to have their shit together? Maybe because they're living my dream? Or maybe it's because they're just arseholes.

With all good intentions, it's still pretty tough to schedule even just a chat nowadays.

You spend at least 6 weeks trying to arrange a date you can both do, and on the fateful day (if you both make it out of the house on time without some kind of bodily fluid-related accident) you'll spend three hours together, yet somehow, not manage to reach the end of a conversation.

One kid is destined to crap themselves just as you get into a juicy bit of gossip, and you're guaranteed to have the other child faceplant the floor and burst into tears as your mate starts opening up about her marriage breakdown.

It's nigh on impossible to look sympathetic whilst subtly trying to console a screaming child in front of a packed-out Pizza Express.

Meeting up with friends who don't have kids is my absolute favourite though. They turn up with their straightened hair and their little clutch bags filled with nothingness.

A beautiful juxtaposition to me; carrying more junk than a council bin lorry after Christmas and wearing half a Rusk in my unwashed mane.

With visions of Insta-worthy baby cuddles, the friend is enthusiastic on arrival; muttering compliments to the baby, who immediately bursts into tears because today they've decided they don't like it when people make eye contact with them.

So, I spend the rest of the outing stood near the table, bouncing up and down repeatedly in an attempt to get the baby to shut the hell up before I burst into flames from the scalding glares coming from my fellow diners.

I'll be honest with you now, if you've been out with me and Isabelle together, I have no idea what you said in response to me shouting '*and how's work?* I'm sorry.

The alternative would be to meet up without the children, but you're guaranteed that the mum will turn up late because their husband conveniently got stuck in traffic for two hours.

When she finally gets there, she spends all night checking her phone to make sure that the kid, or more likely their father, hasn't died out of their care.

So instead, we just send WhatsApp messages saying how much we need to catch up, over and over until one of us dies.

C-SECTION

As I mentioned earlier in the book, I had a planned (elective) caesarean section because of breech presentation, and I really struggled to come to terms with the perceived loss of a natural birth.

There will always be 'those women' out there who will make you feel less of a mother for not tearing your arse out whilst birthing your child, as if we had the choice (and if you do have a choice, pick what is best for you; it's your kid, your body, your recovery and your life).

You know the type; those who compete with how long their labour was or how little pain relief they had, as if BIRFTAs are a thing.

I've even had men - you know the ones whose only job it is to spunk in all of this? - asking me whether I was 'too posh to push', and suggesting that a sun-roof delivery was the easy way out.

I'm not here to compare or compete with anyone, but I will say that c-section birth mothers are no less of a mum than those who birthed vaginally.

The recovery is difficult; they cut through 7 layers of skin and muscle before they even reach the kid, and then each and every one of those layers needs stitching back up again, leaving you doubled over in pain whenever you laugh, sneeze or cough, oh, and a massive scar on your tummy like you've sunburnt the top of your bikini line.

I think people forget that it's major abdominal surgery. I couldn't get out of bed on my own for weeks after my op, but instead of bedrest, I was given a human to keep alive with my tits alone.

This isn't written to scare the shit out of any prospective mothers, I'm just having a hormonal rant and I can't think of anything to shout at Danny for.

Whilst I can't comment on the recovery post-vaginal birth, I'm hazarding a guess that having your lady bits stretch to 10 times their size and then squeezing an actual person out of them is no walk in the park either.

I've seen friends squirm as they perch their arse on a Paw Patrol inflatable swimming ring because they can't sit down: girls who have literally ripped themselves a new arsehole and been discharged home, with no pain relief, the same day.

Women are incredible no matter what their birth story entails. Each one goes through it all for the love of a tiny person (or people) that they haven't even met yet.

We need to empower each and every woman to celebrate their birth story, not use it as bait to make someone feel like she's failed because she had more drugs or a bit of help along the way.

Mothers should be so unbelievably proud of what they have done – growing another human and getting it out of them alive – no matter how they did it.

After the initial wobble I had when I first found out about my need for a section, I decided to change my mindset in an attempt to make the most of the situation I had found myself in.

I asked the consultant whether we could film the birth – not for the feint-hearted – and we dropped the drapes so that we could watch the action as it happened (like Casualty, but the blood and gore is real, and it's coming from inside your own body).

It was the most remarkable day of my life and was honestly an incredibly beautiful birth experience that I would recommend to anyone. I can't wait to freak her out with the video evidence when she's older.

D

Daddy's Home

The single best time of the day. Not just because I can finally have that wee that I've held in since 11am but because its bloody lovely watching her face light up as Daddy walks into the room: she thinks the world of him.

On some days though – the ones where napping isn't cool or teeth decide to grow - Daddy's return can't come quick enough.

There is a reason that Tipping Point is on at 4pm – it's exactly the time that mothers around the country will lose their shit if their partner doesn't tap in pronto.

So, here's a bit of advice to new daddies: if you're running late, it'd be wise to turn up with a box of cremé eggs, a smile and a kiss for both of us, because some days, we've been counting down to your return since 8.30am.

DRESSING

This isn't about dressing yourself - Lord knows that's a shit storm nowadays. If you're new to dressing another human, especially a micro-one, you'll have an absolute ball in those first few weeks.

Their delicate little arms and floppy heads require such caution and tenderness (despite them nearly ripping her head off during birth and her coming out completely unscathed) it took ages for us both to put on her teeny nappy, then vest, then t-shirt, then dress.

Of course, she would then crap herself almost immediately, because parenthood is literally *shits and giggles*.

At the time I'd be furious, but looking back, they were the good old days. Now she screams the house down whenever we put her arms in, as if I'm waterboarding her favourite teddy.

Oh, and a newborn doesn't move. Nowadays, it's like wrestling a mad man into a straight-jacket. Inevitably, my little bugger wriggles free and then crawls away; exposing her skinny bum to the room and leaving a lukewarm liquid trail in her wake.

Dignity

Despite knowing that the maternity team have seen thousands of fannies during their career (and possibly beyond), it still seems odd that a complete stranger can waltz in, mutter their name and within minutes, stick their fingers up your muff (flashbacks to Fresher's week?).

As I had a planned birth (odd turn of phrase, as if some mums have the option of leaving the kid in there), I was spared the regular dilation checks during labour (literally where someone sees how many fingers they can fit inside you like some freakish Bangkok showpiece), but I did have half a dozen strangers staring at my paralysed, naked body from behind a screen, so I wasn't entirely spared the shame.

Caesareans also come with the joy that is catheterisation; a tube wedged up into your bladder to stop you wetting your knickers like a potty-training toddler. How to go from glam MILF to Granny in 60 seconds.

The catheter, the stitches and the lochia (your post-birth bleed) needs checking regularly, which meant that a lovely lady called Becky would pop over to my bed-space every hour or so, lift the covers and stare at my vagina, all whilst I still couldn't feel a damn thing from the boobs down, nor bend in half to have a glimpse at what was so intriguing to her.

 The embarrassment doesn't end when you come home from hospital either. The day after discharge, the midwife visits to check you've all survived the night, though conveniently she doesn't give a time.

When she turned up, I casually mentioned that I wanted to breastfeed but was struggling to hand express and I couldn't bear the pain that accompanied that little alien sucking on my bleeding, shiny-raw nipples. Within seconds, my bra was off and a middle-aged woman was milking me like a cow in front of Philip and Holly. My poor husband didn't know where to look.

Drip, Drip, Dripping

One of the most pointless exercises as a new mum is showering. Not only because it involves effort and contributes to the ever-expanding pile of damn washing, but because, within seconds of stepping out, you're guaranteed to be covered in bodily fluids all over again. If not from a pukey baby, it's from your leaking nipples and bleeding vagina. Sounds gross I know, and it is.

In fact, it's a phenomenal pitch for the new poster campaign for Durex.

DUMMIES

What a blessing from above. The closest you will get to an off-switch (kids don't come with one, I've searched for it. Twice).

Obviously, the misery mafia will tell you it'll be a nightmare to get them off it, but I figured it's not like they're hard drugs. And without one, I reckon I'd have contemplated just that.

And in response to the scare-mongering Dummy Police, Isabelle actually ended up with a horrendous cold over winter which resulted in her self-weaning from the dummy in order to breathe. Every cloud...

It did get me thinking whether holding a kid's nose is an ethical way to wean off dummies, but my legal team - if I had paid for one - would probably advise that I tell you it's not, so don't try.

E

EXHAUSTION

I'm tired. Praise to the mamas who have done this twice. To the ones without a partner. The ones without family nearby.

Praise to the mamas with twins, triplets and more. To the mamas who've got two under two.

To the mamas who have poorly children. The mamas who work full-time. Praise to the mamas who work at all.

Truthfully, I have no idea how you all do it. Some days I can't be arsed to have a shower and I eat biscuits for breakfast and dinner, because you know what? Being a mum is mental.

Yesterday, after toast for breakfast (what a treat) I asked Danny whether the birds would eat the crusts (after the whole 'ducks can't eat bread, yes they can' debacle I'm not up with the current recommendations for ave ingestion). Anyway, he said yes, so I proceeded to throw them out of the patio door, along with the plate, which smashed into a thousand pieces on the flags. I swear I'm losing my mind.

I've accidentally shouted 'Alexa just eat the fucking porridge' because I'm so tired I've confused my own daughter with a sodding house robot.

Some nights Isabelle will wake every hour. She doesn't care if it's a weekend and she certainly didn't give two hoots when the clocks went back. Sleep deprivation has been widely used as a form of enhanced interrogation, and is often considered torture. The problem is, I don't know what information she wants me to give up.

Good-willed people will suggest ridiculously unhelpful things, like *'sleep when the baby sleeps'.* Firstly, it's frowned upon to nap in ASDA, and it's illegal on the M57.

I'll get her back for it one day though. It may be 10 years from now, it may be 20. Sometimes, I make myself smile just imagining me hoovering 15-year old Isabelle's bedroom at 6am, the morning after she's had the girls round for a sleepover.

Oh, and I'll definitely be coming into 21-year old Isabelle's room in the middle of the night for a snuggle between her and her partner, kicking and screaming when they try and put me back in my own bed.

For now though Isabelle, you win, my love.

EXPRESSING

Breastfeeding is beautiful (once you get past the mastitis, cracked nipples and initial pain that makes you want to claw your daughter's face off). And whilst I was driven to give Isabelle 'Mama's best', I knew I'd have just thrown in the towel in those first few days if I had to continue with the pain.

I have no issues with using formula (other than the kitchen worktops permanently giving off an 'upmarket crack den' vibe), but I wanted my supply to stay high, and I really wanted feeding to work, so I chose to express really early on - like, day 2. Against everyone's wishes (despite it being my baby and my boobs).

Truth is, my nipples had never worked as udders before, so they hurt. A lot. Like stubbing your tit on an upturned plug.

Expressing worked for me in those early days because my shiny raw nipple was cocooned inside the breast shield, safely tucked away from any gummy little monsters. Then, when I felt like I was ready, I moved back to the babe on the boob.

I did hate my first pump though. Whoever said 'don't cry over spilt milk' has never had to sit attached to a mains socket for 45 minutes holding what sounds like an old office 3 in 1 printer next to their chest, only to drop the entire bottle on the bastard couch.

I nearly sucked it out to give to her.

4 or 5 spillages later, Danny (fearing for his life) strapped the contraption to my chest with dressing gown belt and piece of rope – more M&S than S&M.

A week or so later, I found myself rocking in time with the pump suction, so I decided to invest in a silent, wearable device. On the whole, it was phenomenal; other than my enormous, Madonna-esque flashing titties which attracted a few admirers in Debenhams (multi-tasking FTW). Still though, breastmilk in a bottle meant that Mama's dairy farm could shut shop every once in a while, for a much-needed full-night's kip. And that is what dreams are made of.

Fear

Science is insane. Mothers have an innate fear for the lives of their children. I'm not talking hand-holding at the roadside or strapping them in on a rollercoaster (those these things are recommended) I'm talking a deep, keep-you-up-in-the-night-even-when-the-little-sod-is-fast-asleep fear of them stopping breathing at any given moment.

This is almost definitely exacerbated by midwives educating parents about Sudden Infant Death Syndrome (SIDS), the sudden unexplained death of a child under one, often in their sleep.

As a result, you spend half the night rocking them to sleep and the other half hovering dangerously close over them to make sure they'll wake up. Inevitably, you accidentally rouse the little monster and have to start the performance all over again. No wonder we're all knackered.

FEET

Here's a fun post-partum fact; your feet go absolutely minging. I'm not sure whether it's because you haven't been able to physically see or touch them for the last two months of pregnancy, or whether it's another hormonal treat, but the hard skin would break an industrial cheese grater.

Fingernails

Because babies do fuck all, their nails grow ridiculously fast. At least twice a week the little buggers need cutting, and in our house, it's down to Mama.

When she was first born you could bite her nails off, which was a pretty easy task considering she didn't move and slept all day.

Now though, you've got absolutely no chance when she's awake, lest she kick you straight in the face or grab the clippers off you and force them into her mouth.

So, it's a stealth get-her-while-she-sleeps job, and there is nothing more terrifying than trying to do a full mani-pedi on a ticking time bomb. One flinch by either of you and you'll clip her precious little skin, and worse than that, you'll wake the devil.

But it must be done. The alternative isn't worth the grief. The kid either claws her own face and it looks like she's been mauled by a cat, or she rips your face off.

Fingerprints

They're everywhere. I'm not talking about the cute ones they make at nursery for Mother's Day, I'm talking about the grubby ones that reflect off the mirror or the sticky ones in the back of the car: the reason we can't have nice things.

First Period

This isn't a flashback to when I was 13, nobody wants to know about that. I'm talking about the first proper period after birth.

You know the one that you've built up to for at least 10 months (or in my case, 10 long, dry years). I wasn't sure whether I had severed some kind of vaginal artery but I called a priest for my last rites.

I know I'd had the lochia (basically a month-long period where blood and gunk come out, alongside bits of uterus and any implements left inside after a section) straight after birth, but somehow (magic happy hormones? The novelty of a brand-new baby? The then not-so distant memory of when I wasn't dead behind the eyes?) I didn't seem phased by that.

This time though, I've got the skin of a teenager and have eaten a 4-pack of Crunchies, three Easter eggs and an entire chocolate fudge cake in two days (though I refuse to believe that diet and dermatology are related: no matter how many people want to ruin chocolate for me).

Anyway, I needed it. I was traumatised after trying to change a sodden tampon with a one of Snow White's seven dwarfs clambering between my squatted legs and pulling at the string like a blood-soaked party popper.

Friendships

Parenthood is intense. More intense than I could ever have imagined, even right up until the day I gave birth. From the moment the baby is placed in your arms, you're smothered with emotion: pride, guilt, fear and love.

You want to have the space in your mind for work and friends and socialising and personal hygiene and giving a shit about anything that anyone else does in their life, but the truth is, in those first few months, you just can't.

Time stops in the rest of the world. That tiny little bundle takes up all the space in your heart and your head, and for me, before I knew it, some of my closest friendships had slipped away.

It was never my intention to lose friends, I guess it just happened. One day, you're you (albeit a rounder, more short-tempered version), and the next, you're Mum. It hits you like a tonne of bricks.

Everything changes, and whilst the 'Old You' is still there somewhere, it's definitely hidden under mounds of washing and dirty nappies.

It's not my friends' fault. They don't get it and I didn't either.

Ashamedly, before Isabelle, a part of me thought that stay-at-home-mum life was for lazy women who didn't want a career. I thought I had it tough working full-time and doing the rest of life outside of the 9 to 5.

I didn't realise that their job was 168 hours a week with no bonuses or overtime, with a boss who screams hysterically whenever you leave the room. No union would stand for that.

Even in the weeks leading up to her birth, I thought that maternity leave would be filled with afternoon tea and play dates on the lawn, that I'd have a huge circle of New Mum friends, and when I wasn't with them, I'd bake or get a new hobby. I had no doubt that I'd be able to keep in touch with everyone because I had an open diary.

Except I don't. Some days I can't be bothered to get dressed. On other days, when I can muster up the energy to leave the house, Isabelle craps through every layer of her outfit five minutes before we were due to leave.

And even if you manage to get passed all of that and get to your lunch date, the baby is still there. There are no breaks. You are always Mum.

I guess I want to say that I'm sorry to the friendships that I've lost or left behind. I'm sorry to the friends who were going through their own shit show and I didn't even realise because I was too wrapped up in mine to notice.

Becoming a Mum made me lose touch with reality because she needed me, and that pressure was and still is intense and all-consuming.

I'm sorry that I was annoyed when friends without kids would complain that they were tired. I honestly thought that they didn't know a damn thing about tiredness, as if nothing in the world was harder than this. I'd be furious when friends socialised without me, though I knew that I wouldn't go even if they asked: insulted that they thought I would leave the baby.

I guess, in this crazy baby bubble, you forget that the real world still turns for everyone else. And what's more, I'm really sorry to the girls who've become a mum before me; those who have lived through this insanity and I've watched on from a distance and not truly supported the way I should have. The way I would now.

Finally, thank you to the friends who stepped up. The ones who saw me drowning and brought me dinner. The ones who sent me for a bath and Danny for a nap whilst they watched the baby. The ones who changed the nappies when I couldn't get on the floor, and who laughed with me when they were doused in piss.

It's true that you learn who your friends are when you have a baby, and I'm really grateful for the ones who didn't bail when I lost a bit of me.

G

GIFTS

Wow, people are so generous when a baby is born! We are really fortunate; Isabelle received countless lovely gifts, some from people I had never even met before.

It was so thoughtful, and really restored my faith in the kindness of strangers.

However.

Please can we all start using common sense. I couldn't have made it simpler; Isabelle was born exactly 6 months away from Christmas day. She's practically slap-bang in the middle of the year, and yet people didn't seem to grasp the whole seasonal sizing thing.

What am I meant to do with a Tiny Baby sized full-length fleecy baby grow for a kid born in June? Who thought she would wear shorts in January? I sound ungrateful and I am. Weather-confused morons.

GOLDEN HOUR

This has nothing to do with sunsets (you'll be too busy wrestling a stray razor off a kid in the bath to watch the sun setting).

It's actually the magical time just after her bedtime and before mine. Phenomenal, life-altering things are planned in this hour; it's when I maintain friendships, socialise, reverse the chaos from the day and restore some kind of order in my home, keep my marriage from the brink of despair, call my mum, perform life admin, meal prep and maybe even have a wash.

Well. Those are my intentions, but I'm knackered, so instead I spend those precious minutes semi-conscious on the couch in front of some drivel like Love Island and promise myself I'll be a better grown-up tomorrow.

Occasionally, you may get a golden hour in the day (usually the time immediately following the 90 minutes spent feeding, rocking and singing to an exhausted yet infuriatingly stubborn baby).

When they finally cave, you're torn between consoling yourself with a multipack of chocolate fingers, attempting to finish painting the garden fence that's been left two-tone for weeks, or doing something even more productive, like showering, for example.

My productivity is directly negatively-correlated with how traumatic the 'settling' phase is; often resulting in even more guilt when she wakes and I realise I've wasted 150 precious minutes doing a *'Which Disney Princess are you?'* quiz on Buzzfeed.

GROWING

I know I sound like your Dad's mate from work, but kids genuinely do grow so fast.

I'm fully qualified to work back of house at a charity shop with the clothes-sorting experience I've gained on mat leave.

Don't bother buying more than a few items per size, and please don't buy expensive brands; kids will shit just as much in Armani as they do in Primarni.

I've somehow managed to accumulate a loft-full of baby clothes that she has already outgrown. I'm keeping them for the next one…you know, if I ever fall onto my head, get trauma-induced amnesia and forget what an absolute shit show this is.

H

HAIR

Isabelle was born with a head full of thick, beautiful brunette hair.

Well, it was beautiful, until clever Mummy here washed almost every lock of it off in the bath.

Within minutes my beautiful brown-haired girl was bald. I mean really bald; like smooth, freshly-bicced, Mitchell Brothers bald. I could see my reflection in the top of her head. All that was left were little tufts around her ears which made her look like a baby Gandhi.

I was mortified; I didn't even crack a smile when my sister in law sent a look-alike collage of her and Shawn Wallace.

But as they say, 'hair grows'. And thankfully, she only had to wear a hat in public for a month or so before this white blonde, untamable fluff appeared. Now, she's the spitting image of Boris Johnson. I think I preferred Gandhi.

Holidays

Before Isabelle was born, Danny and I would go on 3-4 holidays a year. We're not snobs, we just loved to find cheap deals and made a pact that we would never waste a day's annual leave in this country. It was 'our thing'.

So, when Isabelle came along, we agreed we wouldn't let having a baby stop us from doing what we loved.

With a dangerous mix of happy hormones and a few spare hours to kill on a night feed, I found myself booking a cruise for the three of us, for the week after she turned 6 months old.

Strangely, cruises don't let babies younger than six months old onboard; maybe it's something to do with the crying all night. LOL if they think that that stops at six months.

We had already booked a break away with Danny's parents and family for his Mum's 50th, but with that we had the comfort of knowing that there were 11 other people – also known as babysitters - on the plane and in the same villa as us for a week.

The cruise was our first holiday going it alone. So naturally, I invited a load of friends and passed it off as a birthday surprise for Danny.

'Not just a pretty face' you may think, but despite having 12 grown adults in Isabelle's entourage, we still managed to leave her changing bag on the minibus within half an hour of us landing at Barcelona airport.

Other than momentarily displacing everything she owns; the break was a success.

It helped that she was a dream on the plane. Whether it was the movement as we taxied or the drugs that we ploughed her with (I'm kidding, whiskey isn't a drug), she slept from the moment we took off until the moment we landed.

It's bound to come back and bite us on the arse but for now I'm going to enjoy the 5 minutes of gloating.

Only really to spite the snooty businessmen who rolled their eyes and muttered under their breath when they saw us walking towards their seats on the plane.

The biggest adjustment of them all was having to carry a military tour's worth of baby paraphernalia for a human that's smaller than my forearm to survive for a week, as if no other country had ever reared a child before.

Turns out they do sell nappies abroad, but I'd still prefer to take seven packs of our own, just in case we got delayed (for a month or two).

HOT DRINKS

Ah the good old days. I'd recommend you get used to cold coffee or the zesty sting of a water infection because you'll never drink a warm drink again. In fact, I can't remember the last time I didn't have a piss the colour of Lucozade.

Foolishly I spent the first 4 months of maternity leave grabbing a brew and a biscuit in the morning, only to bring it into the living room and get distracted by the stench of a fresh turd or vomit on the carpet.

No bother, I'd just reheat the brew (two hours later) in the microwave.

Only when Danny got home from work and was warming the veg would he find my drink still in there, and I'd realise I hadn't drunk since 9pm the night before. I'd always eat the biscuit though. Fat girls for life.

9 months in and I've finally managed to squeeze a brew in in the morning, I just need to strap Isabelle in the highchair and tell Alexa to play at volume 7 so I can't hear her whining.

Karma bit me on the arse though; this morning I found a bogie stuck to the inside of the mug, after I'd drank half of it. Yummy.

I

Injections

Undoubtedly, immunisations are one of the most important gifts you can give your child, and worth every second of torture (not for her I must add, she forgot about it almost instantly, but for me). That piercing cry broke my heart, but think about it, an afternoon in your pyjamas watching trashy TV and having cuddles with a sleepy, clingy baby? I was asking the nurse whether there were any other jabs I could sign her up for.

Internet

At one time, there were a handful of parenting books, a health visitor telephone number and your own intuition when it came to raising a child. And kids survived.

Nowadays, the world is littered with websites, blogs and vlogs on how to smash motherhood. The only problem is, these keyboard Hunz often have no childcare credentials beyond the fact that they popped their kid out two months before you did.

That doesn't make you an expert, Courtney.

 (And before you say it, I've already told you this isn't a parenting manual: Lord knows I haven't the faintest fuck what I'm doing).

But, come on: there needs to be a ban on girls called Toni-Ann from posting advice on Facebook forums, and Mumsnet members should be forced to list their IQ before they can join.

I learned my lesson when our 10-day old Isabelle was constipated and I had tried all the tricks in the book: bicycle legs, tummy massage, the lot. We even massaged her little bum hole with warm cotton wool like Dr Google said.

Nothing was working, and her screaming was breaking my heart. Sensible Mama-me called the ward and asked for advice, listing all our previous endeavours and praying for an answer. The midwife, yes, a qualified midwife from the ward that birthed my daughter, told me to give her cooled boiled water.

This isn't usually recommended as it fills up little tummies but lacks nutrients, but as she was full to the brim, they suggested that it may help her on her way to a poop - and save our sanity and bleeding ears.

We tried, and 10 minutes later, impatient silly-sod, naïve Mama-me went onto a Facebook newborn support group to find the next solution:

again, listing all of our endeavours and the midwife's suggestion. Some trollop called Helen, whose bio was 'LiVe, LaUgH, LoVe', commented back immediately, 'God Hun you really shouldn't be giving your daughter water.'

No advice, no support, just her high horse opinion. It really upset me, so I made the decision right then to boycott these sites, and somehow Isabelle has made it (relatively unscathed) to her first birthday. So fuck you, Helen.

Invisibility

Remember that fun, hypothetical conversation you used to have with your friends where you would pick what superpower you would have? Well mine was always invisibility.

And SURPRISE! It turns out that when you have a kid your superpower wish is granted, and I'm now invisible to most people.

Nobody says 'hi' to you anymore when you walk into a room and the smile on their face is certainly not for you. Whilst I know I sound like a sad-case, I'm not looking for sympathy.

Just maybe next time you see a mum and baby, acknowledge the mama too (she's the one behind, attached to, or covered in the bodily fluids of the baby).

If I'd have known that wishes came true, I'd have asked for a cellulite removal cream that actually works, and a self-cleaning kitchen floor.

J

JEALOUSY

This is tough to write. Ever since I was a little girl, Granny would say, 'never ever be jealous of anyone'. It's always stuck with me, so if ever that emotion starts to rear its ugly head, I've fought to ignore it.

After all, what reason do I have to be jealous? On paper I've got the perfect life: a gorgeous husband, a beautiful healthy daughter, a supportive family, a nice house and car, and a decent job.

Many people would say I have nothing to be jealous of, and they would be right. But some days, I can't help but feel fleeting pangs of the green stuff.

At times, I'm jealous that my husband gets to go to work. I don't necessarily envy his job or his 7am start, but I'm jealous that he gets to have his lunch, and a shit, in peace.

Other days, I'm jealous of my friends who work for cool companies that travel the globe, and I work my arse off for an NHS that can't even afford to provide PostIt notes anymore.

Since I've become a mother, I've become an ugly kind of jealous. A guilt-ridden jealousy that only a mother can feel; knowing that every negative thought should be quashed by an overwhelming feeling of blessedness.

Knowing that you should always remember that you have never been happier than this moment.

 And yet:

- Some days I'm jealous that I can't book a last-minute trip to the Maldives, because a 24-hour flight with a baby is unfair on her and torture for me (and because I pay two mortgages, one for my house and one for bloody nursery).

- Some days I'm jealous that my friends can up and leave their careers to go backpacking, even though I know I'd rather shit in my hands and clap than carry one of those body bags around with me between 'Gap Yar'-infested hostels.

- Some days I'm jealous of the girls whose bodies have not been ruined by a pregnancy.

And yes, she is my world, but I'm human, and that is how I feel, on some days.

JUDGEMENT

People are always going to judge your parenting decisions. We've all done it before, and subliminally we all do it more often than we would care to admit.

Breast or bottle? Own room or co-sleep? Sling, carrier or your own damn arms? Baby-led weaning, traditional weaning or combi? Sleep-train or wing it? Implement routine or let the baby find their own? God, people will judge you on your drink choice at the damn play centre.

The truth is, for every option above, we all have a different viewpoint on what's best and what's definitely not for us.

You will have acknowledged these without even realising when you read that paragraph. And it is absolutely fine that our answers may be different. My issue is when people thrust their views in my face and suggest that their way is the only way.

Whilst I'd like to think that I'm pretty headstrong, the incessant comments and one-upmanship can wear you down, which is infuriating because as a mother, you and only you (OK, and Dad) know what is best for your child, even if you feel like you've been winging it since you met them.

It makes me so sad when other mums feel the need to defend every decision they make regarding their own baby.

I've noticed it so many times; incredible mothers desperately trying to justify why they aren't breastfeeding their child, mums who say 'she came into my bed last night, but it was only for an hour'. Who the hell am I to judge? Who the hell are any of us to judge?

There is no hard and fast rule on how to bring up a kid and they definitely don't come with a parenting manual (I looked for it when I was trying to find the off-switch).

Ultimately, people will judge you no matter what you do. So, stop giving a shit. And when you find out how, let me know.

K

KIDS

I can't stand other people's kids. Oops, I said it. I'm sorry. But come on, you know the ones I'm talking about; the ones that put their grubby Wotsit-fingers on the pram blanket or who steal the only toy that shuts your baby up for 5 minutes while you have a brew. You know the kid I'm talking about, that one with crisp in their hair and that sticky grey fluff stuff on their face.

They're hard-faced too and always come without a parent in sight.

Kids' parties are the worst. How I wish I could fast-forward the next few years with their shitty-themed fancy dress and inconvenient timing in the middle of a Saturday afternoon.

I'm convinced that we could end teen pregnancy by exposing high school kids to the confines of a church hall and a load of three-year old brats hyped on sugar.

Just the thought makes me shudder.

I don't hate all kids though. I have a soft spot for the Whinge-Bag. You know, the kid that elongates all their vowels and complains how life isn't fair (you've got no fucking idea, mate). But, if I'm honest, its only because it makes me feel warm inside knowing that, for once, Isabelle isn't the dick.

L

LABELS

It's 2020. There's a nuclear apocalypse*. My daughter has still, somehow, managed to find the only label left on the planet, and is sucking it within an inch of its life. The little freak absolutely loves a label.

*Ironically, this section was written before the actual apocalypse of 2020.

Lanugo

Foetuses are covered in a fine hair called lanugo, often nicknamed 'monkey hair'. Though it usually disappears before birth, some children are born with patches of it on their body.

Like our Isabelle, who had hairy shoulders for 2 weeks; not a great look in the middle of summer, Hun.

Leakages

Remember when you were young and your fake Aunty would always say, 'God hasn't she grown?' as if you'd stay the same size forever. Well now I'm that prick; the one who can't believe that kids grow.

I remember saying to my Mum, 'but how will I know when to move her up a size in nappies?'

Let me tell you how you'll know.

A mum friend and I decided to meet in Cheshire Oaks for a bit of retail therapy, lunch and a catch up (only one in every 100 days on maternity leave is like this, and it takes six months of planning and three failed attempts).

With two sleeping babes in their prams, we indulged in carb-heaven, believing that we were smashing mum-life as ladies that lunch.

That was until a whiff of the vinegar shits cast over us. In that situation, you secretly pray it's the other kid. I mean, I love his mum, but it's every mama for themselves on Shit Street.

Of course, it was my kid. It's always my kid. And this was pretty spectacular if I do say so myself. She had shat out of her overly snug nappy, through every layer of her outfit and somehow infused her excrement into the fabric of the pram.

(Massive kudos to my friend who cleaned the whole pram with anti-bac wipes whilst I sorted the shit storm. Not all heroes wear capes).

I don't know if you've ever carried a ball of shit across a restaurant, but it's difficult to do it discretely, especially when the ball of shit is screaming at the top of their lungs like they've just watched Peppa Pig trot into an abattoir.

The bathroom looked like the inside of a student's microwave as the squirming, screaming shitting machine swung off my nipple while I wrestled on the floor with the changing mat.

Who the fuck designed changing rooms without a table? People without children. That's who. Safe to say that wearing a white top wasn't my smartest move; talk about a tiger earning their stripes. I'm just glad that we didn't get forcibly removed from Pizza Express.

But why stop at one shit storm? The following weekend, Mum, Granny, Isabelle and I visited the garden centre to enjoy some fourth-generation bonding time.

My mum adores Isabelle and loved showing her all the over-priced tat on offer.

Until she sharted so violently (Isabelle, not my mum) it blew out through the foot of her leggings and sprayed masala-esque shit all over my mum's shirt dress.

So, if you've started spotting more explosives than a bomb dog, it's time to move up a size.

Lists

Gone are the days of colour-coded bullet journals with calligraphy titles and pretty doodles. But I'd still advise trying to make some kind of list to focus your energy on during nap time (TikTok videos / napping / eating / Instagram stalking all count as valid options).

Otherwise, you end up going upstairs to get the baby monitor, spotting a pile of washing, taking it downstairs and hearing the postman so you pick up the letters and notice that your car tax is due. You open the laptop to renew the tax and find an email from payroll requesting your number, so you go upstairs to find a payslip, notice the file is unorganised and pull all of the papers out, then need a wee.

You spot that the sink needs cleaning so go downstairs to get a cloth and remember the washing you'd left by the door, so you pick it up and whilst doing so, see litter in your garden so you go out to pick that up and then spot Brenda from number 40, have a chat with her for 20 minutes and then realise you hadn't switched the monitor on so run back into the house to cries from a baby who is now wide awake and ready to play again.

Fail.

Today I wrote 3 things to do on my list, and only managed two*:

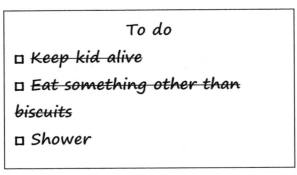

*doughnuts aren't biscuits

LOVE

There is nothing more irritating than a mother telling you 'oh you'll never know a love like it' when talking about their child.

And, though it genuinely makes me wince saying it, I finally understand what they are talking about.

The intensity of love is almost painful. It's not just a little flutter, it's an overwhelming pride; a smothering, suffocating fear, a dogged determination to do all you can to protect them and give them the world.

It's the excruciating pull in your chest when they scream out in pain: it's the way your world lifts and the clouds part when they giggle. It's the boundless joy that they bring, the reason that you didn't smother them in their sleep after they kept you awake all night.

It's the reason that you didn't leave them on the 92 bus when they screamed for the entire big shop, threw your make-up bag into the toilet and showed the postman your nipple. It truly is something else.

Maybe exhaustion makes us think silly thoughts, but I'd do anything for that kid. I thought I knew love before I met her, but I had no idea.

Madness

I still don't think I've quite grasped the fact that I grew a human: a whole other, fully-formed person who lived inside of me, and then got cut out of my stomach like an alien autopsy. It's mental.

I know I'm 29, and I get the whole 'birds and the bees' thing, but, it's still insane that there is another person on this planet, specifically in my damn bed, because of Danny and I (and some clever doctors who know how to cut kids out of people).

I don't believe that you are ever 'ready' for a kid. God, me and Danny had fertility treatment for Isabelle and we still have bleach in a child-lock free cupboard under the kitchen sink and our medicines are kept in a Haribo sweet box. We're useless.

Yet somehow, she's here (and still alive, whoop whoop). She doesn't particularly look like me, unless she gives me a snarl and I instantly recognise her resting bitch face as my own. And her snotty-arse attitude is definitely her Mamas. One thing we have yet to get our head round is the fact that she lives with us full-time.

Sometimes I just look at her and think '*Bloody hell you live here now don't you?*'. And she's not going anywhere: just staying here forever, and it's our responsibility to keep her alive. Madness.

MESSY PLAY

Which prick invented messy play? Yes, Sandra, I'm sure it's phenomenal for her fine motor development and her sensory stimulation blah blah blah, but come on, I can't get the smell of beans out of the carpet and I'm still finding multi-coloured porridge oats scattered around the house as if we have a teeny leprechaun lodger with a bowel condition.

Water play isn't all it's cracked up to be either; I thought she would love splashing in a bowl of water but she just picked it up, drenched herself in it and then cried.

When I put a bit of fairy liquid on her highchair to make bubbles, she sucked them off her fingers and started foaming at the mouth...literally.

And I don't want to be a misery arse when it comes to all this, but she genuinely doesn't give two hoots. I set it all up; pom poms, tinsel, glitter, pipe cleaners, the lot, and she took one look at it, scowled at me and continued smashing the TV remote onto the coffee table and licking the soil off my trainers. Feral child.

MILESTONES

If you've ever read a parenting book (apart from this one, I don't give a shit about milestones) you'll see that kids absolutely, indefinitely, without a doubt, must achieve certain skills at particular ages. Rolling, for example, is expected around 4 months.

The problem is, when people say that, even when you're adamant that you will not succumb to the textbook demands, you subliminally put the pressure on for your kid to do it.

It ruins all of the good stuff that's happening right in front of you, because you're always wishing for the next milestone to be conquered. Yes, I got a buzz the first time she rolled, but I do miss the days when I could leave her on the changing table without her attempting to kamikaze off it (I should probably add that you shouldn't ever leave a kid on a changing table. I definitely never did. Ever).

Michael McIntyre discussed these parenting pressures in his stand up, stating that 'you don't see grown adults crawling into wine bars'. Clearly, he hasn't been to Liverpool on a Saturday afternoon.

MUM-BORES

I've become a Mum-bore. You know those irritating women who show you their entire camera roll of random ugly kids that you don't know or give a flying crap about?

'Oh, and here is one of her sneezing' 'Oh look, this is one of her poo face, how cute is that?' That's me.

I've become that knob head. And I know, like I've done a million times myself, that the response is always an awkward 'aww' – nothing more, nothing less. But still, I just can't stop myself.

I talk about her incessantly, even though I don't particularly want a reaction and I find it awkward knowing how to respond to compliments about her.

The kid could shake a rattle and I'd burst with pride, and even though kids half her age have been doing the same for months, I still have the uncontrollable urge to tell the world just how wonderful my daughter is. It makes me feel a bit sick just saying it.

I'm pretty sure even Danny thinks I've lost it. Last week I sent him a picture with the caption 'Whoop! Her first solid shit!', alongside a picture of just that. A poo. Even her dad won't want to see that on his dinner break.

My Instagram story is littered with videos of her doing absolutely fuck all. I've become the person I hate on social media.

Still, it's better than #furbabies

MUM FRIENDS

I have made some pretty amazing friends whilst off on maternity leave. Naturally, I've gravitated towards the ones who compete only with how shit their night's sleep was, and whose kid is a bigger arsehole.

I tried the whole 'Tinder for Mums' thing online, but all of the women on the apps tended to be boasters or fun-hoovers, and whilst I'm definitely guilty of one too many baby-spam Facebook posts, I need friends who can hold a conversation - even if it takes 3 hours and a well-timed nap or two.

MUSLIN CLOTHS

They're just fancy thin tea towels used as spit rags:

 a) to clean up sick

b) to protect clothing from said sick

 c) to reluctantly hide bosom when teen male cousin is visiting and freaks the hell out at the mere glimpse of side boob (as if his phone isn't full of them).

For some reason, everyone buys you them when the baby is born, and as a result, I have around 40 stashed in her wardrobe. I guess I probably should have been using them instead of my sleeve?

Word of caution: autocorrect will screw you over if you ever text about finding a 'mouldy muslin covered in bits of fluff behind the couch'.

MYTHS

Myths are common-knowledge lies that people tell you to make you feel better. Like horrendous morning sickness being the sign of a healthy baby or that pregnancy glow exists. Well sorry, but I'm not about that life, so here are the cold hard facts dispelling the myths that were told to me:

1)   Breastfeeding helps you to lose weight: bollocks it does. I gained half a stone in the first few months, and that's definitely nothing to do with the packet of chocolate digestives I'd polish off during a cluster feed Netflix binge.

2)   You'll miss these moments: nope. Not all of them I won't. Like the ones where I have poo smeared under my fingernails.

Or the ones where I'm crying because she's crying and it's not her nappy, food, teeth, wind or tiredness (it's all well and good telling me I'll know what the cries mean, but she didn't come with instructions, so I don't).

Or the bleeding nipples. Or the bastard hourly night feeds. OK, so maybe I shouldn't have shouted 'I should be crying not you' at her, but it's really not all sunshine and rainbows, no matter what Instagram says.

3)   Nothing lasts forever: it bloody does. The pile of washing does. The damn dishes do. Being a mum does. But it is precious. Honest.

N

Nap Time

The glorious haven in the middle of the day where you can breathe without a little person swinging off your leg. Well, it was.

Until at 5 months, she decided that naps weren't cool anymore and point blank refused to take them, even though she was visibly exhausted and an absolute crank as a result.

I swear, if someone said *'here we go sweetheart, come and have a lie down, I'll make you a nice drink and I'll even stroke your hair,'* I'd be in bed quicker than you can say *'go the fuck to sleep'*.

I've figured out that she will fall and stay asleep on me, so I'm currently trying to master transferring her into a low cot without waking her, dropping her or falling in after her.

I've done it a few times and fucked it up by celebrating or making myself laugh by creeping out of the room like the Pink Panther.

NAPPY BINS AND BABY CHANGING

Nothing in this world will prepare you for the stench of a nappy bin. Imagine the fumes from a vomit-covered rotting carcass tossed in bin juice. Well, I would douse myself in that to mask the smell of a nappy bin. God bless the poor bastard who empties them.

I swear whatever comes from them is more lethal than any pandemic - never mind Coronavirus, Matt Hancock needs to be sending Hazmat suits to baby changing rooms.

On that note, I wonder how often those rank little changing tables are cleaned?

They're putrid; stained orange (vinegar shits ahoy) and have weird black scratch marks like Satan himself had tried to claw his way out of there.

On yesterday's pull-down-of-doom, I spotted a piece of ham wedged in amongst the hinges. As if the mother had thought, 'Oh here looks like a nice little spot for lunch'. And why not, Isabelle certainly thought it was an ideal place to chow down on the safety strap, with that ham for dessert.

Also, please can they just stop only putting them in the women's toilets? Danny uses it as a get-out every single time; inevitably leaving this lone warrior to save our kamikaze kid from re-ingesting yesterday's dinner.

NAPPY-FREE TIME

As a 21st century Supermum, I obviously conform to all of the current 'Mum trends' [hair flip], including nappy-free time. As it suggests, this is part of the day without their nappy on, as sitting in your own piss can't be pleasant and it makes their little bum skin all chapped.

Common sense. The problem is, to conform to the trend, you have to leave your kid without a nappy on, and even if you tell them not to piss on the floor, they're going to piss on the floor.

Isabelle loves nappy-free time though; kicking her legs in the air full of the joys of spring, and as I thought I'd cracked the pissue (see what I did there?) by putting a towel underneath her, I thought I'd leave her playing and take the dishes into the kitchen. Cocky Mum points.

Sadly, a towel does little for shit, which she managed to smother herself and the carpet in in the 10 seconds I was out of the room.

Where do you start with something like that? Straight in the bath you might say, and I thought that too. Turns out it's not that simple when you're restraining the child from sucking her shit-covered fingers whilst she slips out of your shit-covered hands. We looked like we'd started a food fight in Taste of India, and lost.

Cocky Mum 0, Isabelle 1.

NIGHT SWEATS

Not one person told me about this. A couple of nights into parenthood, your body thinks that the exhaustion, bleeding nipples and sabotaged core is simply not enough, so it sends in the night sweats.

This is the real deal: the bedding was so sodden I genuinely didn't know whether my bladder had exploded or I was bleeding out.

NURSERY

The fear is real. I want her to integrate and socialise but it aches knowing that she's not going to be with me every day.

How do you even begin to find someone to trust with your absolute world?

 Initially we went with proximity: lovely place, nice staff, £62 a day. For that price I'd expect them to wipe her arse with gold-plated toilet paper and serve mashed caviar for morning snack, not a bunch of snot-nosed kids licking communal toys and drinking from the same Tommee Tippee cups.

Then we looked at Ofsted reports (#Mumgoals over here). Truth is though, when it comes down to it, I just wanted someone to love her. Someone who would snuggle her and laugh with her and play peekaboo for an hour and a half and act like they're enjoying it half as much as she is.

We found a lovely place not too far away, and I guess I feel excited for her and the next chapter, even if selfishly I want all of the firsts for myself. She starts next month.

I'm not going to pretend I'm not dreading it, but unfortunately, money doesn't grow on trees, and Santander won't waive my mortgage payments for the next 4 years.

So, if the secret millionaire is around Warrington way (and still alive?), feel free to pop by, I'll put the kettle on.

NURSERY RHYMES

This is an international warning to all new parents. Some prick has changed all of the well-known and well-loved lyrics to every nursery rhyme you've ever known. I'm not kidding.

One of the *wheels on the bus* gets a flat tyre*, *baa baa black sheep* goes into space and someone has added elbows to *Heads, Shoulders, Knees and Toes.* WTF. Oh, and speaking of that, I'm sick of her looking at me like she's been violated whenever I do *Heads, Shoulders, Knees and Toes* on her body. Talk about the kettle calling the pot black.

*Spoiler alert: conveniently, there are animals on the bus who must be studying for an NVQ as Bus Transit Technicians as they all know how to replace a tyre. The elephant and the lion work together and soon the bus is back roaming all through the town, thanks to the trusty lion apparently shouting 'jack it up' to the elephant, not 'off' as I'd be singing for months.

I wasn't impressed to find that you can now *row row row your boat* gently down the stream, creak, river, to the shore and round the bay. I'm all for travelling young but my arms were knackered after that, because let's be honest, the kid doesn't pull their weight at all.

There are also a few new quirky ones about elephants balancing on string (not realistic), and some guy pulling his little lever. Hmm.

Of them all though, my favourite has to be *'Goosey Goosey Gander, where is Amanda?'* - my mother in law.

Though I jest, I do love a good nursery rhyme sing-a-long with her in the car. She laughs at my silly (yet completely safe and responsible) behind-the-wheel dancing (only when we are at traffic lights or when the vehicle is completely stationary, of course) and I love making her smile.

What I'm not so keen on is making the white van man next to me smile when he catches a glimpse of my theatricals, unknowingly performed for his eyes only, as Isabelle has fallen asleep in the back.

O

ON THE MOVE

At 7 months, the whole parenting game cranked up a level as Isabelle started to crawl. It's like living an immersive reality experience of your Hazard Perception test, except instead of you sitting on your arse and clicking a button, you have to run at the fucking danger. Oh, how every last person loves to tell you, 'it's when the fun starts', with their sarcastic little smiles and their distant memories of sticky fingerprints on the TV and bumps to the head.

I'd wished for this day for months: waving toys just out of reach in the hope that she'd clamber over to me on all fours.

And now, I'd give my right arm for one more week with her furiously trapped in one position: incapable of emptying my washing basket, jumping off the changing table or eating a dead fly she's found behind the couch in the conservatory.

I did enjoy the process towards crawling. There was a particular sweet spot when she had only mastered crawling backwards and was forever wedging herself under the couch or the TV stand. I probably should have stopped filming when she was whinging for help, but I've put it down as character building.

It was super cute the first time she pulled herself to stand independently. I was so proud I could have cried. But now, honestly, it's just inconvenient.

There isn't a surface in the house that's safe to put a drink, adding further to the risk factors for death by dehydration, and she's guaranteed to fall and smack her head the one time I leave the room for a wee.

If the Amazon guy knocks on the door when I'm upstairs, you know that parcel is going back to the depot because there is no way I can put on a bra, clamber through three baby gates and find my front door keys in time.

I get that they're meant to keep the kid from falling to their death, but we're more likely to end up in A&E because I've stubbed my fucking toe on that bar across the bottom, again.

Nobody warns you how quickly it'll all happen either (OK, so every man and his dog warn you, but you don't listen). One day she was a useless, immobile little alien.

The next, I'm glancing at the monitor and she's stood up with her head partly wedged between the bars like the Great chuffa chuffa choo choo

Train Robber himself.

I used to pray for silence, but now, it only means that she's causing havoc; probably chomping on a plug or gnawing the hair off my brush.

She found her stride at 10 months, and there is honestly nothing more disturbing than watching your baby morph into a small, pissed old man stumbling around the living room shouting slurs at *Mickey Mouse Clubhouse.*

Oops

I've finally taught Isabelle how to wave - hooray, I'm so proud. Well, I was. You see, her attempts were enthusiastic to begin with, but now they've become half-arsed, and by half-arsed, I mean a fucking Nazi salute.

OVERHANG

Put on your sultry voice because we are going to do a little mindfulness exercise.

Imagine your partner has whisked you away to a remote desert island with swaying palm trees and crystal-clear waters. He's packed a bag for your stay, with your favourite costume and flip flops.

He's even remembered to bring entertainment for the beach. Inside the bag you spot your favourite book (ahem...), a lilo, and a beach ball. Now imagine the beach ball.

Picture opening that tiny little cardboard box that it comes in and remove the ball to inflate it. Now what would you do with the box?

Because let's be honest, no matter how hard you try, that ball is never going back inside that box.

To cut a long story short, I'm the fucking beach ball. Those jeans are not going back on my friend, and it's because of this bastard overhang.

An overhang is basically a kangaroo pouch without the slit at the top. Don't bother googling it, all that comes up are pages and pages of motivational shit from yummy mummies who 'bounced back' with 'a balanced diet and exercise'. Just wear high waisted jeans and comfort eat like the rest of us.

PATIENCE

You've not known patience until you have become a mother. Good Lord, I would have throttled this child if she wasn't my own.

Danny, on the other hand, loses his shit within 5 minutes of her becoming a crank, which, as you'll know if you've met Isabelle, is around 5 times a day.

I would be lying if I said that my patience didn't wear thin on some days though: like when she continually launches her toys off the highchair tray, and then screams because all of her toys are out of reach on the floor.

Or when she wails every single time she has to put a vest on as if I'm attempting to suffocate her, though I've never done it. I've not even tried. It's like she has the memory of a goldfish, or a sleep-deprived mother.

I've cleaned the bastard kitchen floor 4 times today, and I'll do it again tomorrow, and yet she cries at me like I'm the one taking the piss. I'm telling you if this is a sign of things to come in Toddlerdom, I'd like to know the returns policy please.

PEEKABOO

For a 6-month old, Peekaboo is comedy gold. Not only does it help to build an understanding of fancy things like object permanence, shared communication, consistency and contingency, but it also keeps her entertained for at least three minutes, with gorgeous belly-laughs every single time you pop out from behind your hands. As a scouser, our version of Peekaboo is 'I see'. Same premise, but instead we say 'I see', because, well, we see them. It makes sense. Scouse logic.

As it happens, there are hundreds of titles for this one game; prompting an intense debate with my in-laws, who call it everything from 'Peepo' to 'Hideyboo' (what?). It turns out Isabelle couldn't care less what you say; every single one makes her laugh as long as you disappear and come back again. Easy win.

Oh, apart from the day we booked a £250 photoshoot. Ironically, that was the day that not one of the hundreds of Peekaboo variants was even slightly amusing anymore. FML.

PELVIC FLOOR

Ah the pelvic floor. The blessing we didn't know we had. The reason we can hold a wee in for longer than 15 seconds, and the reason you don't see mums on trampolines.

Post-baby, every laugh, cough and sneeze pose a flood risk, so you are kindly reminded to practice pelvic floor exercises during and post-pregnancy to save yourself from a life of Tena Lady.

Adam Kay, in his phenomenal book 'This is going to hurt' beautifully described this exercise as *'sitting in a bath of eels and trying to not let any get in'.*

PERINEUM

I was blissfully unaware of the meaning of this word until I entered my third trimester. Before that, it was just a mysterious place that the back of Veet told me I shouldn't wax.

Oh, how I miss the naivety.

My first real eye-opener was during an ante-natal class with Danny and six others couples at our local hospital. The true reality of pregnancy and birth set in when the midwife recommended that we started perineal massage every night in preparation.

Danny and I looked at one another, the curiosity and excitement in his face suggesting that he thought a perineal massage was some sort of romantic hot stone affair for the both of us. He certainly didn't think he would be fumbling around rubbing his wife's gooch in an attempt to stretch it and stop it ripping her a uni-hole.

Thank god for my breech baby.

Poo

Mature, I know, but we have to talk about poo. How can something so delicate and beautifully fragile produce something so offensive?

Let's start at the start. Meconium. Google image that now if you don't know what it is. What an absolute post-birth treat that is (1-0 to the section girls who thankfully couldn't feel their legs to get out of bed and change that one).

Then there are the chicken tikka vinegar shits. They're often a fluorescent orange (perfect for staining baby clothes) and occasionally tinged with green (like that moss that grows on patio flags in the winter).

Your midwife will tell you to wipe a girl's bum from front to back; as if there isn't already half a tonne of shit encrusted into her ladybits. Anyway, the chicken tikka poos last a while, and on special occasions come with bits, though nobody really knows why.

When you start introducing food, you get the glorious semi-solid weaning poos. There is no greater reality check than wiping someone else's actual big-girl shit off your hand, especially when they come with a literal reminder of what she's had for dinner. Tip: If you've given your child red pepper, it's courtesy to inform the nappy changer who otherwise would definitely think that the baby has passed massive clumps of blood in their poo and call an ambulance.

God bless the reusable-nappy mamas - absolute saints. I realised that other day that I'm so used to bags of shit lying around my house now that I barely even notice them.

I'm mortified just at the thought of an unexpected visitor having to tip-toe over the excrement landmines I've planted in the hall. Unless they, like my husband, can't see them either.

POPPERS

Ah poppers: little pissing press studs of misery. Parents are so exhausted and subsequently moronic that the clothing companies have even changed the colour of one popper to indicate a start point, yet somehow, I think I'm better than this and as a result, spend half my day popping press studs closed and then ripping them back open again because there's a gaping hole by her bum.

And how do you spot a childless clothes designer?

Buttons.

Q

QUESTIONS

Small talk is the bane of my life.

Yes, Carol from number 44, the weather is miserable, it's always fucking miserable.

Yes, Mr. Waiter, I am just out doing a bit of shopping, why on Earth else would I be in Cheshire Oaks on a Saturday?

Leave me alone.

The wretchedness really cranks up a notch with a baby though. Now I can't even make eye contact with a stranger without superficial chit-chat, and it's always the same 5 questions:

Is she good?

Oh yes, last night she did a sponsored sleep out for the homeless and she's been nominated for a Pride of Britain Award for her work with vulnerable adults.

How old?

29 and a quarter. Oh, you mean her?

Does she sleep?

Yep, every time we go to any one of the classes that I've paid a shit tonne of money for. Other than that, no not really. That's why I look like I'm terminally ill.

Isn't she lovely?

You don't have to live with her and her sass Stevie.

Is it your first?

*No, no I've actually got...oh bollocks they've gone *run away feigning panic**

end of conversation.

The one that really boils my blood is:

So, when are you going to have another?

1. Why, what's wrong with this one?
2. That's such a personal question, how do you even know if we can?
3. My scar has barely healed, give me a break
4. One kid is expensive, noisy, dirty and messy enough

5. I'm genuinely not even sure if we like this
   one yet

R

Random Shit

I'd love to be a fly on the wall in the house of a new mum. Surely I'm not the only one who spends her day trying to get the baby to do pointless things.

I swear I've lost countless precious hours attempting to get this kid, who frankly couldn't give a shit, to show me 'how big' she is.

Neither does she wants to clap her damn hands, which, because another kid at playgroup can do it, has been our focus all bloody week.

'Clap hands. Isabelle clap hands. Clap. Clap. Clap. Clap. Ohhh clap hands. Isabelle. Isabelle. Isabelle. Clap hands. Clap Hands Isabelle. Claaapppp hands, Daddy come. I don't know the words. Clap clap. Clap your hands like me. Oh, forget it'

Relationships

Babies change everything, and it's no wonder why. Pre-baby I'd never watched my husband suck snot out of someone else's nose, and I'd get the girls out on a special occasion, not in Debenhams café or in front of his Grandad Dave.

It's not that the romance is dead, just maybe comatose.

There's nothing like shit on your arm to ruin the mood, which even if you push past that will still inevitably end with a not-so-perfectly timed interruption from the baby monitor.

'Maybe tomorrow love'.

It's tough. I think, secretly, we're both grieving for the partners we had before she was born; the spontaneous, showered, shaven other-half.

I miss the effort we used to make for each other; the tickle fights and the little notes on the sideboard. I miss when sleeping next to him wasn't a fucking luxury.

I can't deny that she has brought more love into this family than we could have ever imagined, and I wouldn't change her for the world.

However, I would be lying if I didn't acknowledge that the impact a newborn has had on our lives has been overwhelming at times, because no matter how hard you try, you change.

You both get sucked into a swirling vortex of tummy time and sterilising and your brain can't focus on anything other than when she last shat.

I can't remember the last time we had a decent conversation about something that wasn't Isabelle, and sometimes, that's suffocating.

After a lot of tears and snappy, exhaustion-fueled arguments, we both agreed that we needed to make a conscious effort to find us again. Not Mummy and Daddy, but Bec and Dan. It's easy to say it now, but it had taken us 7 months to even realise that we were lost.

S

Separation Anxiety

Another beautiful yet suffocating developmental phase happens at around 7 months, when the kid realises that despite everyone being genuinely lovely to her, she couldn't give two shits and wants to be with, and only with, her mother.

She screams when you leave the room, and clings tightly onto you like a little chimp whenever another human dares to look at her. It's precious, and only ever so slightly irritating.

Shopping

I'm talking about food shopping, because I'd rather tweeze my own nipple hair than shop for clothes to suit this muffin top.

I often walk over to ASDA with Isabelle in the pram (usually for a creme egg or five). With no time constraints and eyes bigger than my semi-deflated helium balloon of a belly, I always end up picking up half a week's worth of stuff, which, even after eight months off, I haven't managed to master carrying around the shop. I've tried all below, with limited success:

a)   Carry it all in one hand and try to push the pram with the other. Outcome: dropped a pack of apples which rolled in opposite directions all over the floor.

b)   Basket and pram. Outcome: no hands left for actual shopping, and a basket indentation on your forearm.

c)   Perch the items on the sleeping baby leaving me hands-free to browse at ease. Outcome: wakes the kid every time and results in me having to panic feed her in the rancid baby changing cubicle or paying for a cup of dishwater that they pass off as a brew in the café. No thanks.

d)   Put the shopping under the pram pre-checkout. Outcome: I can't relax the entire shopping experience because I feel horrendous guilt about sneaking items into my pram basket as if I'm a low-grade criminal. I try to compensate by being sickeningly overfriendly to all the staff members in an attempt to convince them that I'm not a hardened chocolate thief.

The only day I felt as though I mastered it was when I'd invented a grapefruit holder with a bra I'd picked up in George; I was delighted that they weren't kiwis or easy-peel satsumas.

(Edit: I've stopped breastfeeding and they're now like pears).

SICKNESS

I think she's had a cold since she was born. But you can't win; you either sterilise everything within an inch of its life and then she practically dies when she goes to nursery, or you spend your maternity leave covered in snot and being coughed at in the face.

I chose the latter, in the hope that she would build up her immunity (and that the snuffly times would make her nap time longer so I could get a washload done). Also, poorly baby snuggles are everything.

Sleep

Fuck. Me. This kid does not sleep. And the loving family-focused little darling has taken us on the misery train with her. For the past 8 months.

8 months.

Just think about to how knackered you are the day after a heavy night on the piss. Think about feeling that tired, cumulatively, for 8 fucking months.

Then ask Alexa to play 'screaming baby' on Spotify, and listen to that over and over and over until eventually you lose your mind. That's parenthood.

Some mothers (the ones with the curly blows and the smug look on their face) are lucky - their precious little shit apparently slept through from 4 weeks old.

I call bullshit. They definitely put the kid in the garden or slipped a Rohypnol in their Cow & Gate.

People say 'breastfed babies get up more often in the night'. So, we tested the theory and made her long-arm 8oz of formula at bedtime. The little shit still woke four times, like some kind of cuckoo clock in a torture chamber.

For a while, we even trialled a deep squat bouncing ritual in the desperate hope of promoting some shut eye.

Think Monica from Friends '*woah baby baby baby*' but performed by a Boltonian joiner at his wit's end.

Her Dad's motion sickness mustn't be hereditary though, as somehow, she found being flung around the living room relaxing. It got her off to sleep every time.

Maybe the movement reminded her of the comfort she felt inside her mother's womb, or maybe the G-force knocked her out – either way, it worked. The workout with an 18lb screaming dumbbell wasn't ideal, but it was worth it for the hours of golden silence that followed.

We thought we had cracked it, but even that bliss was short-lived. People go on about sleep regressions but I reckon she's either nocturnal or she's broken. There is no other option.

I've thought about keeping her awake all day long, but she just screams and screams like a banshee. We've used lullabies, white noise, cot mobiles, a freaking light show above her bed, and nothing works.

And yet, whenever the little sod stays at her grandparents, she will sleep the whole night through. Cow.

She's even taken to refusing to go back to sleep in her cot from around 5 in the morning; knowing that her desperate parents will let her stay in their bed if that grants them a couple more hours shut-eye. We know it's not ideal, but at 5am, I'd shoot a kitten to get another hour in.

I still haven't quite got used to her there, and subsequently shit myself every morning as I wake to the sound of her muttering in parseltongue while pulling on my nostrils. I've started bringing a toy into the room with us so that after she's woken me, she can wake her Daddy by smashing that in his face. Again, it doesn't provide me with any more sleep, but it's funny as fuck.

Sniff test

I grieve for the time when I didn't smell a stain to see whether it was chocolate or shit, or rub her nappy and smell my fingers.

Soft Play

My idea of hell on earth. A germ-ridden sweat bucket that smells like sick and feet, with Baby Shark playing on repeat until your ears bleed.

I thought it'd be the perfect place to let her burn off some steam, but as it turns out, she can't even walk, so I have to crawl between the sensory toys with my arse hanging out of the jeans that I'm determined to fit into.

She's too young to go on any of the actual soft play; on the one day we tried it I nearly ended up punching a kid for knocking her over, so we stick to the free sensory class upstairs. It's crap, but the hot chocolates are decent.

Inevitably, you end up having to make small talk with other mums; namely the one whose kid keeps prodding you in the back.

Nothing like a forced relationship with another human based solely on the fact that you have bonked at the same time (ask Danny).

It's also worth going to people watch. Honestly, you really do see everything in these places; last week there was a woman who hand-expressed a full 9oz bottle whilst eating a panini. Seriously impressive.

SPEECH

As a Speech and Language Therapist, her communication development is paramount to me. I've spoken and sang to her every day, and even before she was born, I'd play music to her in the womb and she would flutter about in excitement.

 I'm such an advocate for story-time and read to her daily. I narrate my day and shower her with words wherever we go.

And what word does she say first? Fucking *Dada*.

Dad, Daddy, Dada, DAAAAAAAAAAAD.

Has she said Mama yet? No. Not even once. Though I'm about 95% sure that she says *shit*. In context too. Oops.

SWIMMING

I love our swimming class. Aside from it costing more than my bastard mortgage each month, it's half an hour of golden bonding time. Oh, and it makes her sleep all afternoon so Mama can catch up on 'housework' (The Apprentice/Bake Off/dead scrolling on Facebook).

Great idea in principle; baby learns to swim, saves her own life when she inevitably falls in a swimming pool or gets swept away at sea. Key life skill taught before she's one; just call me Supermum. In reality though, most of the lessons were spent either 'bounce-bouncing-this-a-way', or dunking the poor kid underwater.

For the first term she absolutely hated it and would scream for most of the session. Spot the worst Mum in the world.

Luckily, she loves it now (well, she's stopped the screaming and might even crack a smile on occasion), so that's £160 a term well spent.

I jest, I'm actually so proud of her development in the pool. She now holds on to the wall after she's fallen into the water, a skill that could potentially save her life. How incredible. Only caveat is that I have to sing 'Humpty Dumpty had a great fall' before she falls in.

Swimming also comes with the need to get practically naked in front of a group of strangers each week, which in my pre-Mama life would involve a full de-fuzz and a week of gradual tan in prep.

It's funny how quickly the enthusiasm to rock a hairless bod wanes when you're running on 3 hours' sleep and a quick pits and bits shower with an (often impatient) audience.

Instead, I've mastered the quickest slippery-floor-walk from the changing room cubicle to the pool. God help me if another mum ever brushes up against me in a class, she'd think Lassie was drowning.

Strength

Christ, where do kids get their brute strength from? Sod Britain's Strongest Man, I want to see Britain's Strongest Baby. I can see it now: the heats would be bowl throwing, spoon wrestling and pram resistance, with qualifiers going through to the hair-pull tug o' war semis.

Escape from a nappy change would be the ultimate finale - biggest shit-storm wins.

Thankless

Motherhood can often feel like a thankless task. I'm at peace with her saying *Dada* first (it actually works a bloody treat when I ask her who she wants to change her bum – give the kid what she wants) but I'm not overly thrilled with *garden*, *stuck* and *sweetcorn* making the list before me. She doesn't even like fucking sweetcorn.

And I reckon I've probably changed well over a thousand nappies since she's been here, yet she won't even let me shit in peace: and not once has she offered to wipe for me.

Some days I'll delve into Supermum life and I'll trawl through a weaning recipe book to find something wonderfully nutritious and tasty (using the scraps that are on the verge of rotting in the fridge of course, I'm not a martyr).

Two minutes after serving, she will take a handful and hold it over the side of the highchair.

Making sure I'm watching, and with a facial expression that can only be described as 'disgusted', she will fling the food onto the floor then chuckle, reminding me that:

a)   that was an hour that I'll never get back

b)   I'm her bitch now.

Oh, and my boobs are round my ankles, my tummy looks like a prune and I vomited for 3 months straight because of her, but that's fine sweetie, *you scream at me because I won't give you a slice of melon when you've got seven of your own and you don't even fucking like melon.*
Still, somehow, it's all worth it for her: the little snort when she giggles, the way she smiles at me and her nose wrinkles, the joy on her face the first thing in the morning as she mutters absolute nonsense at me with real intent.
It's madness, and thankless, yet utterly glorious.

Teething

Whoop. I finally felt like I was starting to smash motherhood. Take yesterday for example, both me and the baby had three meals and I even changed my underwear.

So, what did Mother Nature (who is definitely not a Mother because no woman would shit on another's parade like this) do? She sent a little message to Isabelle's gummies to destroy our lives. '*Send in the teeth*'.

Teeth are these teeny little white knives that rip through your baby's perfect little gums and heart. They turn your angel into an absolute arsehole and there is nothing you can do to stop them (and believe me, I tried ALL the drugs).

People say useless things to you too, like 'lots of Mummy cuddles today then'. Well I'm telling you now; Ibuprofen, Calpol, Anbesol and Bonjela simultaneously did fuck all, so unless I cuddle so hard that I accidentally smother her, I doubt that my arms alone will make a dent in breaking through that foul mood.

The pain isn't the only symptom though; they drool everywhere, as if Shamu had mated with a bloodhound. Like pressing on an ulcer, they find relief in chewing on anything they can get their mitts on, well, apart from any of the four teething rings I'd paid six quid each for.

With every tooth, her cheeks flush like the first time I had a smear, prompting everyone to ask *'Oh is she warm? She looks warm. Little rosy red cheeks. Are you sure she's not too warm?'* which, after the fifth time, makes me want to smack an old lady in the face (but I don't, because, well, jail).

Someone was definitely in a dickish mood when they designed kids' teeth. They aren't born with them (OK some are, but that's fucking terrifying) so they (and we) need to endure the pain of every single one of them coming through individually, and then they all fall out because they're fucking useless and aren't actually the teeth they fancy keeping for the rest of their lives.

The parents then need to pay for the privilege of the bastards falling out, which apparently is now at least a pound a tooth, and the whole rigmarole starts again. What a waste of my life.

When the teeth first cut you have to add toothbrushing to the ever-expanding morning and night-time routines. And surprise surprise chuck, she hates that too.

In fact, her toothbrush is probably the only thing in this house that hasn't been in her mouth. Danny had the smart idea of buying an electric brush for her, hoping that this would release the clamp on her teeth whenever we approach.

On it went, and the brush went straight into her mouth - wonderful. Until she tasted the minty freshness and removed it immediately; the vibrating head spraying Colgate across the bathroom like a knock-off foam machine.

THRUSH

Nipple thrush, in fact. So sexy, and itchy.

TIME OUT

She's a little small for the naughty step (though her sassy attitude could benefit from an hour or two with the Supernanny). I'm actually talking about time that we spend away from her.

The beautiful, life-affirming times when Isabelle sleeps over at her grandparents and Danny and I get some precious hours to ourselves. Every parent's dream.

Oh, the quality time we will treasure; rekindling our love and remembering why we actually got together in the first place. The romantic meal we will cook, the washing we will do, the cleaning and life-organising and shopping and meal prepping. The sleeping.

And yet, well, it's just we often get so excited about our freedom to chill that we forget to do anything else. 24 hours later, we resurface from the couch, surrounded by chocolate wrappers and empty coke cans. Best laid plans…

And I miss her terribly when we are apart. I miss her little laugh and the way she grips on so tightly to my hair that she could scalp me in an instant. I miss the snuggles and the accidental head butts that burst a lip – mine, not hers, Officer.

Obviously, as soon as she's home, I'm reminded of the things I don't miss: the brown French polish owing to the shit under my fingernails and the crime scene replica that is, in fact, strawberries smeared onto my kitchen cupboard doors.

On the whole, I guess parenthood is similar to Brits abroad: we crave a break in the sunshine all year, that one week of escapism from the misery of the UK. But, as soon as we get there, we seek out an Irish bar and order a full English and a *Guinness*. We know that something more exotic and exciting is out there, but there's nothing like the comfort of home.

Toys

Nothing tests your patience more than a high-pitched, battery-operated robot repeatedly demanding that you 'sing with me' over and over until you smash her head in with a hardback copy of *The Gruffalo*.

And 'thank you' to all the battery-licking children of the 90s; you're the reason that Mummy needs a tiny screwdriver to euthanise it, and unless it's boxing day, I haven't got a clue where to find one. It's not even like she's interested in playing with real toys. My living room constantly looks like Mr. Tumble's wet dream and yet you can pretty much always find Isabelle sitting in the hall eating a shoe.

This morning she spent a good 15 minutes sucking my blusher brush, I didn't know whether to be furious or to give her the rest and go for a nap.

The worst toys have to be the fabric ones with electronic speech elements. They get covered in snot and food stains within a week, yet you can't wash them in the machine. I know this because I washed Cora, the talking bear, and now she only says 'hello baby' and laughs over and over and over. Either she's sponge-clean only or she's fucking possessed.

TRAPPED

Though I have no work to go to, no rush hour commute, no scheduled meetings or patients to see, some days I find the limitations posed by a tiny human's nap times unbearable.

Some days, I feel like I need to complete the entirety of grown-up life while she's asleep, because I can do fuck all when she's awake.

Like yesterday, I wanted to go into the garden and cut down some trees (it's spring, and a new season makes me slightly crazy like a werewolf or a vampire).

I took Isabelle out, along with a basket full of toys, a little picnic mat, her highchair and a bag of crisps (veggie flavoured ones of course, because I'm a wonderful mother).

Despite enough entertainment to see her through 'til Christmas, she screamed within minutes of being outside.

I tried to tease her into playing with the grass, but she refused to touch it as if we were unknowingly playing a game of 'the floor is lava', and even the crisps weren't distracting her from the misery of being 3ft away from me for 20 seconds.

So, I had no option but to wave the white flag and retreat to our prison cell. Of course, after packing away all of the tools, she no longer wanted to go inside, nor play with me, and was quite content eating a pile of soil.

I reckon I'll just have to give her my undivided attention until she's 18. Only 100 months to go.

TUMMY TIME

Another recommendation that my daughter could not bear to do. Whilst tummy time is meant to strengthen a newborn's neck and back muscles to prepare them for crawling, my daughter spent her tummy time screaming blue murder, face-planting the floor or sucking dirt out of the carpet.

As I'm a model parent, I didn't give up and instead bought her a tummy time roller (second-hand from Facebook Marketplace for £3 of course. I love her but not that much, they cost a fortune brand-new).

Now, instead of screaming into the floor, she screams into the roller, and then rolls off it and screams into the floor. £3 well spent for the comedy roll.

TV

Yes, I was that Mum who was convinced that she wouldn't let her kid watch telly. I swore throughout my pregnancy that I wouldn't tarnish her precious brain with mindless drivel, and I stuck to it for the first few months.

Now? My suggested Top Picks on Sky are *Blue's Clues* and that wretched brat, *Peppa Pig*. But truth be told, you've got to pick your battles. Sometimes, I just want a brew, and sometimes, I just want to change her smelly arse without a shit show on the carpet. And if the *Hot Dog Dance* keeps her still for two minutes, then I'm not above shouting *Oh Toodles!* with Mickey and the gang.

That being said, I'm still pretty sure that the baby does not want to watch *Alaskan Bush People* with her Dad despite his protests, and that that does not constitute 'watching the baby' while I clean the house.

Despite kids' TV providing us with small wins (like a solitary piss) it's still mind-numbing to watch.

Like Norman, the arsonist on *Fireman Sam* – he should be extradited from Pontypandy after all the fires he's started, the little shit. How is he still allowed to live there? Danny and I clashed heads over this, he argued that he is keeping Sam and his chums in a job which ultimately supports the local economy as the council would probably strip the funding otherwise. Absolute bollocks.

One thing I will not watch is *In The Night Garden*. Just the name is creepy; imagine those little freaks running around the patio at all hours of the morning. And they chat shit too.

U

UNDERWEAR

I've never been sexy. In fact, I'm ridiculously unsexy. My idea of dancing is flailing my arms about like one of those tube men outside a car dealership, and I point blank refuse to pay £25 for a skimpy pair of knicks from Victoria Secrets.

But if ever there was a teeny ounce of sensuality in me, it died the day I became a Mum.

You're advised to buy Bridget Jones-style knickers – the bigger the better – following a c-section, to avoid irritating your scar and to ensure that your husband doesn't want to come anywhere near you ever again.

Seven months later, I'm still in them and although I could possibly squeeze into my thongs of old, I'm secretly loving my new comfort-above-everything lifestyle. They even come with the added bonus of consolidating your flab into one neat package, like a pay-day loan. Great.

UNDERWHELM

I expected to feel overwhelmed by #mumlife: the exhaustion, the noise, the mess. I didn't expect to feel massively underwhelmed by the whole experience. In fact, it's this which has prompted me to write this book. I'm bored shitless.

Let me get this clear, I am so grateful to have a daughter. She's genuinely hilarious and her cheeky little face could light up a room. But some days are dull. Some days I can't be fucked to wind the bobbin up anymore.

I'm so tired of pairing up teeny tiny little socks and mashing up dinners (though ironically, this is actually something I do in work too).

I miss conversation and adult humour. I miss challenging myself intellectually, and what's more, I know others must feel this too.

We're surrounded by trolls who force us to feel guilty if we feel anything but infinite joy; who remind us constantly that our children are a blessing and we should enjoy 'every single second'. That some people aren't so fortunate so we should never, ever complain about the privilege that is being a mother.

That is true, we are so, so lucky, but some days are still mind-numbing, and I say that whilst still distinctly remembering the fear of infertility and the journey we went on to get her.

Some of my closest friends have suffered horrendous miscarriages, the pain of which I can't begin to imagine, and whilst I feel guilt even admitting it, deep down I know that it doesn't take anything away from you as a mother to admit that some days you need more than Old McDonald and a cold brew.

UNSOLICITED ADVICE

Everyone - family, friends, fake 'friends' on Facebook, bloggers and vloggers (who the fuck even are they?), Sue from work, the woman behind the checkout in Asda - has got something to say about how, and how not, to bring up your kid.

It doesn't matter how many years ago they had their baby (if they even have one), all and sundry are akin to a qualified midwife, and a mouthy one at that, when conversing with a mother to be:

'She (at 6 weeks old) needs to be started on solids already she's starving'

'Sleep when the baby sleeps'

'Put her down you'll spoil her'

'Dip her dummy in a whiskey' (!)

...the list is endless, and whilst well-meaning, the useful nuggets of advice are often buried in amongst outdated bullshit.

If you had a quid for every time you heard, 'well in my day we didn't do that...' you could have bought that £1500 travel system from Mamas & Papas.

Let me remind you that in their day, smoking was permitted on aeroplanes and their precious little gremlins didn't even have to wear a seatbelt in a moving car.

It's hard enough having to remember and implement all of the professional advice that is thrown at you (honestly, ante-natal classes should be renamed *'100 ways to kill your kid'*)

And if giving god-damn water to your little munchkin is frowned upon, JD and coke is probably not health-visitor approved, despite what your Great-Granny says.

Vinegar shits

Oh, the vinegar shits. The sweet-smelling, eye-burning, fluorescent orange vinegar shits. You'll never fancy fish and chips again.

Visitors

New-Mum life is pretty overwhelming, especially in those early days. It's beautiful, intense, terrifying, and everything in between.

Many friends warned me of the heightened emotions and the impact it has on your new little unit.

They recommended that we took some time to absorb it all as a new family of 3, without opening the door to visitors. Some recommended staying in bed for the first week, others only allowing visitors after their husband's paternity leave had ended.

Whilst I hugely respected their decisions, I knew that our families would be disappointed if I had closed the doors without first allowing a cuddle with their newest edition.

After all, Isabelle had not only given us new titles, but also made parents into grandparents, and siblings into aunts and uncles.

We discussed the option, and whilst it undoubtedly had its appeal, we agreed that we couldn't, and wouldn't deny them that joy. Was it the right decision? I think so. It brought more happiness to our close family than we have ever seen before.

However, the lack of a strict closed-door policy opened the floodgates for many, many more guests. I know that everyone loves a baby. I get it.

But seriously, what lunatic was dishing out privilege passes to the masses on the day my kid was born? It was as if everyone in the land believed that they had a God-given right to snuggles with my brand-new human in the first moments of her life. These people were not best friends or close family members.

They were practically strangers: people from far and wide, some who I haven't seen in years, who would message within hours of her birth suggesting a date for their visit, and I didn't even have their number saved in my phone. I'm talking droves of tea-guzzling, 'oh -I'll -have -a -biscuit -too -if -you -have -any', mummy smotherers. Giddy, cuddle-hungry randomers.

And yet, amidst the exhaustion, the pride and the hormonal overload, I accommodated visits for almost all of them. It's still something I regret to this day.

Why did I let that happen to us? Was I wanting to prove that I could be Supermum: recovering from major abdominal surgery and still playing host to guests with a face full of make-up and biscuits in the tin? I'd like to think so, but sadly, I think I succumbed to the pressure, the Great British illness of politeness at all costs, and the inability to say no.

I guess I'm also a sheep of our generation. Like everybody else, I accede to the pressure of living in a world of social media, which falsifies reality and lets everybody in. I share my life online with everyone from the popular girl in high school to the couple we'd met 8 years ago in Turkey. Maybe, at my most vulnerable time, my online persona blurred the lines between social media 'friends' and the real deal.

Facebook Bex definitely portrayed a woman with her shit together. I posted filtered pictures only on the few days I was dressed and I'd hastily dabbed a bit of foundation on. I fed their belief that I was recovered and that the door was always open for guests.

I never let anyone see me crying for no reason or pumping my engorged breasts until my nipples were raw. Why the fuck would anybody want strangers in their house a week after they've been sawn in half like some shit magician's finale gone wrong?

I know I didn't, and yet, when Isabelle was 6 weeks old, I was broken, sleep-deprived and hormonally overloaded. We had only had 3 days without visitors in that whole time, because I just couldn't say no.

The pressure to accommodate visitors is a feeling often shared by new mums, yet we continue to do it because we always think we can cope. I definitely fell victim to it. In fact, the whole experience made me question what advice I would pass forward to future parents. Should I have listened to the girls who had tried to warn me? Those who knew the vulnerability of post-partum life and the deep desire to bond as a family unit? Maybe.

But more so, I should have acknowledged that opening the door doesn't have to be an all or nothing approach. Having my mum visit – the woman who has seen me at my worst and my best – doesn't mean that I need to host work colleagues or distant family.

Accepting that isn't as easy as it sounds. You will be surprised who wants to make you feel guilty for owning your space. I received a gift in the post from a girl I had met on a hen do when Isabelle was 3 weeks old.

When I text her to say thank you, she responded with *'I had to send it it's been in the house too long'.* One visitor said *'she doesn't do much does she? She will be better when she's about 6 months old'.* If only I'd had the balls to say *'well you can happily fuck off 'til then then'.* Hindsight is a wonderful thing.

If I could go back, I think I would tell myself to stay in bed for a week with no visitors at all. And whilst I can pretend that I would listen, I know that I'd be a huge hypocrite to pass that advice forward. I was told to do exactly that and I ignored it. As will you. You will want to show off that teeny tiny bundle of love to the world. I get it. So instead, here is some advice to pass on to the visitors:

- If you're invited, don't overstay your welcome. I'd honestly had enough of the majority of our guests after about an hour. If you're coming after work, don't stay all bloody night. Routines are a pipedream in those early days but stimulating the baby so late on in the day doesn't bode well for a decent night's kip.

- Mamas are overwhelmed with emotion and will miss their teeny person even if they're still in the room. I've never felt more vulnerable than when I watched people passing her around and felt like I couldn't ask for her back. So, if you're a visitor, ask the mama regularly if she wants baby back for cuddles. And please, if Mum does ask for baby back, don't say stupid comments like 'you get to cuddle her all the time'. Sometimes all the time still isn't enough.

- Babies are amazing. Though they can't talk, they give cues as to what they need. A beautiful example is the rooting reflex, where baby thrusts their tongue and turns their head into the breast. Midwives will advise to feed baby as soon as these cues are spotted to avoid the trauma of a screaming, starving baby. Less stress for baby, less stress for Mama. Win win. Keep a look out for the cues, and give baby back to Mama to feed when they're spotted (or offer to bottle feed).

I've had too many visitors ignoring these cues and some Smart Alecs telling me to wait until she cries before I feed her. They've obviously never tried to latch a screaming baby before. And, on that note, when baby does cry, your bouncing/singing/swinging around the room won't work, my tits will, so hand her over.

- 2 weeks after major abdominal surgery, Mum is not here to host. Make your own brew and make her one too. Oh, and bring biscuits. If you don't feel comfortable making a brew in her house, you shouldn't be there.

- I'm not an obsessive mother. I worked in a hospital and pulled down asbestos ceilings during my pregnancy. That's my decision. However, if you want to hold the baby, wash your damn hands. Oh, and if you're ill, you're not welcome.

- There is nothing better than the scent of a newborn baby. It's like a drug. So, if you have the honour of a snuggle, don't turn up doused in aftershave. You stink, and now so does the baby. Oh, and if you smoke, don't bother coming full stop. Thanks.

- If you wake my sleeping baby you can deal with the aftermath. This may require lactation, so if you can't do that, avoid waking her.

- Be expectant that the parents may cancel your visit last minute. They may change their mind and that is ok. After I had rearranged a visit after a pretty rough night with the baby, a 'friend' messaged back saying 'Oh right, great, was just about to leave'. Don't put guilt on an already overwhelmed Mum.

-Just generally don't be a twat and you'll be fine (food always helps).

W

Washing

Want to kill a polar bear and pay a small fortune each month for energy bills?

Get yourself a newborn. If they haven't shit, pissed or vommed on their outfit, you're guaranteed to drop a freshly-dipped chocolate digestive onto you both, ruining that one 5-minute break you catch all day.

I genuinely think I spend more than Dot Cotton on detergent and am convinced that someone is secretly putting all the freshly-laundered clothes back into the wash basket. In fact, I'm pretty sure it's Danny.

I thought I'd catch a break when she stopped barfing on herself and shitting through her outfits, but then the little bugger started weaning. Don't know if you've ever smeared an Ella's Kitchen pouch into everything you fucking own? Not only do they stink to the high heavens, but they stain like a bitch.

I'm pretty sure I should own honorary shares in Vanish.

WEANING

Weaning is the most remarkable developmental experience. There is nothing quite like watching the excitement on your little one's face as they explore the world of taste for the first time (not a shoe or a leaf, but actual human food), and going on a journey yourself to find the most delicious and nutritious food options for them (until you discover those veg flavoured puffs and figure that a broccoli crisp is definitely the same as the real deal).

There is something so primitive about the satisfaction a mother feels watching her baby enjoy food. Shame the same can't be said for watching their baby smear carrot puree into their eyebrows and up their nose.

God their little fucking noses. Every day she manages to wedge some variety of culinary mush up her nostrils. I wouldn't mind but have you ever tried cleaning a kid's nose? They'll pull out some black belt karate shit quicker than you can say '*Mr. Miyagi on ecstasy*'.

I wasn't a fan of baby-led weaning. I loved the idea (she would be much less likely to get a full carrot baton stuck up her nose) but I actually shat myself and pulled the food from her every time she gagged because I was terrified that I'd have to do back blows on a 6-month old. So, we stuck to the messy mush.

I'm convinced that there are some positives to weaning though, like sleeping more often. I would too if I'd spent 40 minutes burning energy by launching plates off the highchair like a Greek waiter in a bib.

Weaning also eats into your day. Food prep, feeding and cleaning up a massacre swallows a chunk of those 8-hours waiting for the hubby to come home.

Oh, and I don't need to get my boobs out every 20 minutes anymore, which is such a blessing, as she has taken to coming off the boob to have a nosey every time she hears a noise, leaving the old nipple flapping in the wind.

Though I'd still take that over having to wrestle with a pre-toddler to change a weaning poo, which is pretty much an adult shit smeared into her teeny tush and kept warm in her nappy.

I'm just saying I'm not above letting her suck on a hoover nozzle if it means she will just lie still for three minutes.

WEIGH-INS

Going to get the baby weighed is an absolute ball-ache. Especially in the winter. God, you have to wrap them up to take them outside, then strip them entirely in front of a room of people, who probably aren't judging but it definitely feels like they're watching; just waiting for you to accidentally let the kid roll off the mat.

Then you have to sit with a naked human on your lap and wait for the lady to call you over, during which time the baby will definitely piss on your trousers. You finally get called over, and realise you forgot the bastard red book, so the kid can't be weighed anyway.

You leave covered in piss, with a screaming baby whose weight you still don't know, and have to return the following week to do it all again.

Winding

The WORST job ever. Babies need winding all the bloody time, and its bollocks when people say that breastfed babies don't. None of this pathetic tap-tap-tapping either, you've got to put some effort in. It's exhausting!

By week 6 I was pretty much bouncing her off my leg like a bucking broncho in the hope of getting it up so that she could go back to sleep. You see, I've learnt my lesson. I've been cocky one too many times letting her fall asleep mid-feed and putting her back into her cot without the obligatory backrub, fearing that that will only wake her up.

Smugly, I waltz back into bed in the darkness, happy with my minimal effort for maximum gain, only to be woken half an hour later by a screaming misery-arse who now has trapped wind and is all about making me pay for my half-arsed parenting.

Absolute fail.

WINGING IT

I have no idea what I'm doing. Genuinely. Yesterday, Isabelle pulled herself up to standing against the couch. My sister in law and I both thought each other was watching her, and subsequently both looked on as she fell head-first to the floor (builds character though, right?)

I remember thinking when I was little that my Mum was the oracle: a fountain of knowledge and an expert on everything. Now, I'm the Mum. I'm the one who is meant to know stuff and pass it on to her. I'm meant to mould her tiny mind with words and love and experiences so that she grows up to be a loving, thoughtful, intelligent, passionate and driven human being who wants to make the world a better place.

And yet some days, all I want is for her to go to sleep so that I can eat a box of creme eggs and binge watch the Bake Off. I have a genuine fear about how I'll survive when she no longer needs a nap; what will we do all day?

I do wonder whether anyone actually has their shit together or if it's all a pretence.

I'm praying it's all lies, but if it's not, please don't tell me.

WORK

Though I've spent most of my time complaining about the mundanity of it all, I know that I am really lucky to be able to have taken a whole year off with Isabelle.

It's a privilege to have watched her grow from a babe in arms to a fiery, independent and funny little person. That being said, I'm feeling all sorts of emotions about going back.

Practically, just the thought makes me feel sick: how will I get us both dressed, fed and out of the house for 6.30am? How will my brain cope with more information than the number of scoops per fluid oz and the words to The Grand Old Duke of York? How will she cope without me? What if she's fine and I struggle?

I'm certainly not looking forward to the long days and the emotional demands of an acute stroke ward. And I definitely don't fancy sitting in rush-hour traffic with a furious one-year old who is knackered after a day at nursery.

On the whole, I know that it's going to be another uphill battle, but one I need to face. I want her to be inspired by me as a working mama, I want to retain that part of me and my career that took so long to progress towards, and I want a hot brew and adult conversation.

But sadly, the main driving force is not wanting to get my home repossessed because I can't afford the mortgage as stay-at-home-mum isn't a lucrative career option, no matter how appealing it sounds.

Let's be honest, nothing begins with x. She doesn't play the xylophone and hasn't needed an x-ray (yet). So, it's included for completeness (and word count).

Y

You

Nobody told me that I would lose myself. That some days I'd crave my old life and all that came with it. That I'd miss the spontaneity, the freedom and my sense of self. That I'd even miss going to work. Then the mum guilt hits.

 How could I possibly grieve for my old life when I'm meant to be so overwhelmingly besotted with my new, shiny, shit-stained one? People would give anything for the gift of a child, I know, I've been right there in the fertility clinic with the best of them.

But in amongst that infinite love and absolute joy was a little twinge of sadness as I realised that my life has changed immeasurably. Some days, even still, I find it sad that I can't run off to New Zealand to do my PhD, or do another summer working at Disney World. And though Insta Mamas suggest that you 'still can', I'm not sure it'd be the same on 3 hours sleep and a tiny person sucking on your nipples.

I've also changed as a wife. My priority isn't Danny anymore. He isn't my number one. And just writing that makes me cry. I'm too exhausted to make an effort anymore. I snap at him for the smallest of things because I spend all day in the damn shithole of a house – which no matter how often you clean still ends up a bomb site – or surrounded by mums who are just fucking boring.

For the first few months of Isabelle's life, I think we just existed. We survived day-by-day and our communication was purely based around what time the new tenant had woken, fed or shat. I lived on auto-mum mode until I reached breaking point when she was about 3 and a half months old. I couldn't be this baby feeding robot anymore. She would scream constantly and I would cry right alongside her. I wanted out. Not out of her life, just out of the house without a massive bag full of baby shit. Just a shower on my own. Just one full night's sleep.

So, I contacted work and asked if I could do a couple of Keeping in Touch (KIT) days. I contacted my friends and asked them to meet up for tea; without the kids. And I told Danny I needed him at home more.

It wasn't me failing, it was me recognising that I needed to find me again. I love being Mum, but I love it even more when I'm refreshed after a little break. Nobody tells you it's OK to want a break from your kids. Maybe a screaming toddler or a moody-ass teenager. But not a newborn.

But here I was searching for breathing space away from the snuggles of a teeny helpless little person. Not because I didn't love her, but because I remembered that I needed to still love me.

Z

Zaftig

Me 2019-present. Thanks kid.

Epilogue

And just like that, you're one.

First year done, and somehow, we are all still alive. We survived. I'm not going to pretend it's been glorious every day, but, looking back, I'd do it all over again in a heartbeat.

Your sassy attitude and infectious smile bring so much joy into this house; filling a void we didn't even know existed before you.

The way you laugh at your Daddy melts my icy-heart. I've never been happier than when we are dancing together in the kitchen, or having races to see who can get to the flip-flop first.

You've challenged me more than any degree, job or exam ever could, and at some points, I felt like an absolute failure.

But look at you. You're perfect. We must have done something right.

I guess motherhood isn't about smashing it every single day.

It's about surviving one shitastrophe at a time, and doing your absolute best for the little human who thinks the world of you.

And if that's being Supermum, then I guess that's me.

ABOUT THE AUTHOR

Rebecca grew up in Liverpool with her Mum and younger brother. She is now living in Warrington with her childhood sweetheart, Danny, and their daughter Isabelle.

Rebecca works as a Highly Specialist Speech and Language Therapist, and has always loved to write.

Mum's the Word is her first publication, focusing specifically on the trials and tribulations of the first year of parenthood.

She has released a sequel to *Mum's the Word*, with the wonderfully original and highly innovative title, *Mum's the Word 2.* If you haven't bought it yet, ignore the last few pages and get yourself a copy immediately.

Acknowledgements

Firstly, I have to say a huge thank you to everyone who has read and given feedback on the book. Your honesty and words of encouragement pushed me to achieve what has always been a dream of mine.

To Danny – *You're right: opposites do attract. We are so different and yet we complement one another perfectly. Thank you for your patience, your infinite love and for always being on my team. I love being your wife.*

To Mum– *Thanks for showing me what it means to be a mother; you're my cheerleader, my voice of reason and my biggest fan. I'm so proud to be your daughter, and hope that Isabelle and I have a bond like ours.*

To Granny and Grandad – *Your support is unwavering. I am where I am because of you, and I'll be forever grateful for the work ethic you have instilled in me. I love you so much.*

To Adam and Liv – *Thank you for supporting this project right from the start. Liv, thank you for reading and re-reading every single page, your comments are so valued. Adam, thanks for just being your glorious self. Also, thanks for the date nights, we needed them.*

To Amanda and Mark – *I am so proud to be your daughter-in-law. The love and affection you show to Isabelle is second-to-none, and we appreciate you more than you'll ever know.*

To Gem, Rick, Beth and Stacey – *Thanks for always spotting when I am drowning and offering to babysit. You gave me the breathing space I needed.*

To Nikki – *Thanks for sharing maternity leave with me. You have been my soundboard for so many rants, and have provided me with comfort and laughter as we try to figure this shit out together.*

Last Request

If you've made it this far, thank you. My final request is that if you've enjoyed this book, please review it on Amazon and tell your mum friends (and tell them to tell their friends, and maybe their rich Uncle too).

It's pretty tough being a teeny little independent author, so your recommendations mean everything. I'm serious.

Alternatively, order a few hundred copies so that we can finish the en-suite.

AND...if you do the social media thing, come and say HI @bookmumstheword
(I'm on them all, against my will).

FINALLY – *MUM'S THE WORD 2: It's all sh*ts and giggles* is OUT NOW!

Printed in Great Britain
by Amazon

22793061R00126